Poetry 1945 to 1980

LONGMAN ENGLISH SERIES

This series includes both period anthologies and selections from the work of individual authors. The introductions and notes have been based upon the most up-to-date criticism and scholarship and the editors have been chosen for their special knowledge of the material.

General Editor *Maurice Hussey*

Poetry 1945 to 1980

Anthony Thwaite
John Mole

Longman

LONGMAN GROUP LIMITED
Longman House
Burnt Mill, Harlow, Essex CM20 2JE, England
and Associated Companies throughout the world

First published in conjunction with Faber and Faber Ltd 1983
ISBN 0 582 35148 0

Set in Garamond 3 11 on 11 (Linotron 202)
by Syarikat Seng Teik Sdn. Bhd.,
  Kuala Lumpur,
  Malaysia.

Printed in Singapore by
The Print House (Pte) Ltd.

NOTE ON THE EDITORS

Anthony Thwaite was born in 1930. After leaving Oxford he taught English literature for two years at Tokyo University, and since then has been in turn a BBC radio producer, literary editor of *The Listener*, assistant professor of English at the University of Libya, and literary editor of the *New Statesman*. Since 1973 he has been co-editor of *Encounter*. He has published seven books of poems, most recently *Victorian Voices* (Oxford University Press, 1980), three books of criticism, several anthologies, and some travel writing, as well as doing a great deal of reviewing and broadcasting. He has travelled widely for the British Council and other bodies, lecturing and giving readings all over the world.

John Mole was born in 1941 in Taunton, Somerset, and educated at King's School, Bruton, and Magdalene College, Cambridge. He is co-founder and editor of the Mandeville Press, which publishes contemporary poetry in small hand-set editions. He has published five collections of his own poems, the most recent of which is *Feeding the Lake* (Secker and Warburg, 1981). He is a teacher of English and, as a broadcaster, has presented poetry programmes for the BBC. He has also written feature programmes for BBC Schools' *Listening and Writing* and *Books, Plays, Poems*.

Contents

Introduction

All the poems in this anthology were written after the end of the Second World War. The division is of course an artificial and arbitrary one, but then most critical divisions are, even those which may appear tidily to follow preordained chronological limits: 'Poetry of the First World War', 'The Eighteenth-century Novel', 'Painters of the Renaissance', etc. Such divisions may suggest a point of view. To finish an earlier survey in 1914 would suggest an end of innocence, the close of the long Edwardian summer. To begin, as we do, immediately after the Second World War might be seen as representing an even greater watershed – a date beyond which one must learn to live with the numbing recognition of what happened in the concentration camps and in the shadow of the nuclear bomb.

In all the arts, though, shock is often delayed. Occasionally, a work such as Picasso's *Guernica* combines outrage with imaginative control and makes its statement at the heart of the conflict: Picasso painted it soon after the bombing of the Spanish village that gave his work its title. But more often the experience of extreme suffering needs time to find its necessary shape: for example, David Jones's *In Parenthesis*, perhaps the most moving and certainly the most ambitious single literary work to come out of the First World War, yet not published until 1937; or Stanley Spencer's murals in Burghclere Chapel, not completed until 1933. In the same way, much of the poetry which most powerfully draws its imagery from the devastation, holocaust and clinical bestialities of the years 1939–1945 did not begin to appear until the late 1950s.

There were, of course, poets during the Second World War, and many of them, who wrote out of their immediate experience; but whereas the best poets of the First World War, such as Wilfred Owen and Siegfried Sassoon, emphasised the fellowship of suffering (the dominant image being that of the trench, with violence and death at close quarters), many of those who wrote through the Second World War experienced a degree of depersonalisation, whether they were on so-called active service or were bureaucratised civilians. In the words of Stephen Spender, one may detect 'in English poetry of these years the haunting presence of a lament which is really for the lost and neglected freedom of emotion and imagination'. The disillusion and outrage which showed itself in the poetry of the First World

War becomes, in 1939–1945, a kind of level, sane endurance, an acknowledgement of the necessary struggle against Nazism and Fascism but an inability to become part of its Churchillian rhetoric. There was a practical involvement in 'winning the war', but poems often come from the local, frequently frustrating minutiae of day-to-day military or administrative activity, whether in T. S. Eliot's post-air-raid 'dead patrol' with Dante in *Little Gidding* or in Henry Reed's laconic and even satirical 'Naming of Parts'. As Alun Lewis (killed in Burma in 1944) wrote: 'Acceptance seems so spiritless, protest so vain. In between the two I live.'

Against this one should set the solitary supposed literary 'movement' that was identified among British poets in these war years, as the New Apocalypse. The rather absurd title did, it is true, embrace some rather absurd writing: a self-conscious amalgam of Surrealism, Freud, Jung, and old-fashioned romantic sentimentality. It tried to represent a counter-current to what was seen as the too reasonable, too cerebral, privileged upper-class, superciliously social attitudes of Auden and his contemporaries. Such a view of Auden and Co. is too narrow, and it is not a simple matter of one generation replacing another: they were concurrent.

'Historically', G. S. Fraser wrote, 'the 1940s were a broken-up period, five years of war, followed by five or more spartan years of Crippsian peace.' (Cripps was the Chancellor of the Exchequer in the 1945 Labour Government who imposed 'austerity' measures on Britain in an attempt to recover the economy after the devastations and disruptions of war.) The spirit of the post-war years was marked by reconstruction, restraint, sobriety, the sensible. Its attempts at celebration and exuberance, marked in different ways by the 1951 Festival of Britain and such plays of Christopher Fry's as *The Lady's Not For Burning*, now look quaint. More characteristic of the spirit of the time was a mood which, in its literary manifestations, became known as 'the Movement'. This is the subject of a full-length book by Blake Morrison (*The Movement: English poetry and fiction of the 1950s*, Oxford University Press, 1980), which patiently unravels the myths and the realities. Some of its features have been more briefly summed up in Jonathan Raban's *The Society of the Poem* (Harrap, 1971), when he writes:

What has been sought is a voice that has the authenticity and the authority of ordinariness; a language in which daily detail, low-key speech rhythms, and the experience and feeling of Rotherham rather than Byzantium add up to make a rhetoric with which the poem can deal face to face with the middling areas of contemporary society.

If this sounds negative, so it was in some of its results. But the 1956 anthology *New Lines*, edited by Robert Conquest, frequently seen as the manifesto of 'the Movement', brought together such different poets – included in our own anthology – as Philip Larkin and Thom Gunn, whose best work transcends these 'middling areas'.

The presiding figures of T. S. Eliot and W. H. Auden were still there, though Eliot had moved towards writing plays which were scarcely recognisable as 'verse drama' and Auden had long ago removed himself to America. Almost as soon as 'the Movement' had been journalistically identified, some of its members indignantly or truculently denied they had anything to do with it, and at the same time other forces began to make themselves felt. A number of student poets who had regularly met in Cambridge during the mid-1950s to read and discuss one another's work started to follow their livelihoods in London, where they drew a wider clientele into their discussions and became known as 'the Group'. In their Cambridge days Ted Hughes had been one of them, in 1957 he published his first book, *The Hawk in the Rain*, which was an immediate success, being seen by some as a proper corrective to the sort of voice identified by Jonathan Raban in the passage quoted earlier. 'The Group' saw Hughes as a father figure, but the best of those who emerged from its discussions (such as Alan Brownjohn and Peter Porter) seem to have little to do with Hughes's preoccupations.

By the time *A Group Anthology* was published in 1963, the total picture of British poetry looked a great deal more various than it did in the immediate post war period. Philip Larkin and Ted Hughes had established themselves as, if nothing else, the most talked-about talents since Dylan Thomas; and running parallel with Hughes's emergence there began to be an interest in the poetry of other European countries – the recent poetry, arising from wartime occupation and, later, the communist regimes, rather than the earlier aesthetics which helped to shape the Modernist movement of the first decades of the twentieth century. This interest came about through, and with, the wider availability of translations of such East European poets as Miroslav Holub from Czechoslovakia, Zbigniew Herbert from Poland, and Vasko Popa from Yugoslavia. Hughes has helped translate and promote some of this work, and the influence of Holub and, even more, Popa can be seen in his own poems: a kind of hermetic black comedy (to be compared with its increasing popularity in the theatre), a poetry of fragments produced under pressure — though the pressures of postwar Britain have hardly been of the kind experienced by writers under totalitarian regimes.

These European influences were different from those coming in from America in the 1960s, which were broadly of two kinds: 'confessional' poetry, in which the poet tenaciously and remorselessly (but also often remorsefully) worries away at himself; and a kind of freewheeling, sometimes violent, open-structured verse which in America was associated with the 'Beat' movement, having its origin partly in the supposedly relaxed ('laid back') happenings of California, but with some radical political content as well. The confessional mode travelled most readily to Britain in the poems of Robert Lowell, from his *Life Studies* (1959) on. In our anthology it can be seen most brilliantly, and in a voice of its own, in Sylvia Plath, an American who made her reputation first in England, living and dying here. As for the Beats, they surfaced in an oddly diminished fashion on this side of the Atlantic, among what are usually called the 'Pop' poets of the 1960s: what was sometimes genuinely ferocious and anarchic in such Americans as Allen Ginsberg and Gregory Corso became ingratiating and winsome in the voices that started to proclaim and banter from Liverpool; and for this reason we have not represented these over-exposed entertainers, whose entertainment in any case nowadays sounds dated.

But one cannot avoid a whole area which the Pop poets did much to open up: that of poetry readings. From the mid-1960s until now (though the peak of the fashion has receded into the distance) many poets of quite different persuasions have found themselves in front of audiences large and small, in schools, colleges, arts centres and theatres. Television and recordings have spread the audience, ironing out the differences between the kind of entertainer John Betjeman can be and the kinds of comedian Pam Ayres and Spike Milligan are. When a poet faces a live audience, and becomes habituated to it, the temptation is for him to produce poetry *for* performance, rather than to perform poetry: the audience can be wooed, flattered, fed with patter. An article in a recent issue of *Junior Education* has a teacher quoting with apparent approval 'one bright eleven-year-old' who said of some poems by Pop poets: 'They're like telly ads, only not trying to sell you anything.'

The expansion of poetry into areas it had not reached before can, however, be linked with the growth of regionalism within the British Isles in recent years. Many poets have become identified with their own regional areas, and there has been a corresponding proliferation of provincial publishing firms, some of which have become national in importance: Blackstaff, Carcanet, Peterloo. True provincialism does not mean narrowness: it is marked by an energy and imaginative concern which extends far beyond the locality which, in the first place, gives it its strength. Since the late 1960s this has been most true of the remarkable renaissance of literature, particularly poetry, in Northern Ireland. The tensions of Ulster have been accompanied by a shaping spirit represented in our anthology at length in the work of Seamus Heaney. (It is a measure of Ulster's present excellence to say that we regret this single representation: if we had had space, we would have included another half dozen – Michael Longley, Derek Mahon, John Montagu, Paul Muldoon, Frank Ormsby, Tom Paulin.) Heaney's earlier poems, careful re-creations of his upbringing on a small farm in Co. Derry, were probably over-praised, and they were eagerly brought into the schools by teachers who had been influenced by F. R. Leavis's notions of the 'organic community' (further transmitted into the educational system by the writings of Raymond Williams and David Holbrook) and by the same kind of nostalgic urban yearning for the countryside that made these teachers equally keen to entrench Laurie Lee's *Cider with Rosie* in the syllabus, rediscover John Clare and Edward Thomas, and embrace the early 'animal' poems of Ted Hughes. But Heaney has gone well beyond that, using – but not exploiting – a sense of history in his plumbings and delvings.

This sense of history can include the present day, as it does in different ways in Heaney's 'Orange Drums, Tyrone', 'Punishment' and 'The Toome Road'. They use the past to illuminate the present; and this process can be seen at work elsewhere in this anthology. There are the re-creations of Auden's 'The Shield of Achilles', Sylvia Plath's 'Lady Lazarus',

Geoffrey Hill's 'Ovid in the Third Reich' and 'Mercian Hymns'. Personal experience of the Second World War is resurrected, years after the event, in Vernon Scannell's 'Walking Wounded'.

This is only one of the strands one can pick up from the poetry of the 1970s and the present day which we have included, but it is central to the work of three of the most admired poets now: Seamus Heaney, Geoffrey Hill and R. S. Thomas. They seem to answer a need for not only an historical dimension but also a cohesive vision, a generous humanity and an unsentimental stressing of the spiritual. There is nothing unduly solemn about this, though the abstract descriptions may sound so. These three poets are vivid, dense, rewarding, and certainly not unapproachable.

Our anthology is essentially a collection of poets whose work we admire rather than a comprehensive survey of poets we have been afraid to leave out. It would be wrong to see all the poets fitting snugly into the pockets of social history: the two whose work begins the book (Robert Graves and Stevie Smith) escape such classification, as does Craig Raine who concludes it, though it would be fair to comment that Raine's 'Flying to Belfast, 1977' draws on a place grindingly familiar from newspaper headlines in recent years: Ulster. The postwar period has shown an astonishing, even bewildering, variety of styles and manners. No one poet has been dominant in Britain, though it would be conventionally true to say that the work of Dylan Thomas influenced much that was going on in the late 1940s, and that in the 1950s, 1960s and 1970s there was the successive pervasive influence of Philip Larkin and Ted Hughes. We have included several poets not commonly anthologised, as well as leaving out some who are. We are not by nature exclusivists, people who jealously try to guard a small number of the Chosen. We regret the absence of such senior poets as David Jones and Basil Bunting, whose best characteristic work is on a very large scale which can only be damaged by filleting out anthology-scale extracts.

The notes on each poet, and the notes on individual poems at the end of each selection, are there to help the reader make his or her own judgement, to elucidate where elucidation seemed necessary, and to help start the sort of discussion which may never end but which at least ought to begin when one reads a new poem. Nothing is presented as dogmatic.

Anthony Thwaite
John Mole

Robert Graves

Robert Graves was born in 1895, and his education at
Charterhouse, Oxford and, most importantly, in the trenches of
the First World War, is described in his autobiography *Goodbye
to All That*. This remarkable book, combining as it does the
experience of passion with modes of detachment, and treating of
real horrors with a kind of black anecdotal humour, is an early
pointer to what has remained distinctive in Graves's poetry.
Much of his best work is, on the surface, elegant, cool and often
extremely witty. His diction is precise, sometimes suggesting
the clipped tones of an army officer, and his choice of vocabulary
marked by a fastidious classicism. However, within and
between his lines, there runs a subsong of deep feeling, by turns
anxious and celebratory. His total commitment, over the past
thirty years, to the White Goddess – the dangerous, irresistible
poetic Muse – has been pursued in a voluntary Majorcan exile
and has nourished his finest poetry in much the same way as
W. B. Yeats's patterning of thought in *A Vision* did his. Both
poets systematised intuition and scholarship of a bizarre, eclectic
nature into a rich personal myth out of which they came to
speak with authority and to write with the confidence (even the
hauteur) which makes their poetry memorable. It is perhaps
something of a paradox that despite an apparently increasing
eccentricity and isolation marked by indifference or plain
hostility to most of his contemporaries, Graves has continued to
write some of the most approachable and enduring poetry of this
century.

Here Live Your Life Out

Window-gazing, at one time or another
In the course of travel, you must have startled at
Some coign of true felicity. 'Stay!' it beckoned,
'Here live your life out!' If you were simple-hearted
The village rose, perhaps, from a broad stream
Lined with alders and gold-flowering flags –
Hills, hay-fields, orchards, mills – and, plain to see,
The very house behind its mulberry-tree
Stood, by a miracle, untenanted!

Alas, you could not alight, found yourself jolted
Viciously on; public conveyances
Are not amenable to casual halts
Except in sternly drawn emergencies –
Bandits, floods, landslides, earthquakes or the like –
Nor could you muster resolution enough
To shout: 'This is emergency, let me out!',
Rushing to grasp their brakes; so the whole scene
Withdrew for ever. Once at the terminus
(As your internal mentor will have told you),
It would have been pure folly to engage
A private car, drive back, sue for possession.
Too far, too late:
Already bolder tenants were at the gate.

Surgical Ward: Men

Something occurred after the operation
To scare the surgeons (though no fault of theirs),
Whose reassurance did not fool me long.
Beyond the shy, concerned faces of nurses
A single white-hot eye, focusing on me,
Forced sweat in rivers down from scalp to belly.
I whistled, gasped or sang, with blanching knuckles
Clutched at my bed-grip almost till it cracked:
Too proud, still, to let loose Bedlamite screeches
And bring the charge-nurse scuttling down the aisle
With morphia-needle levelled . . .

                                        Lady Morphia —
Her scorpion kiss and dark gyrating dreams —
She in mistrust of whom I dared out-dare,
Two minutes longer than seemed possible,
Pain, that unpurposed, matchless elemental
Stronger than fear or grief, stranger than love.

A Dream of Frances Speedwell

I fell in love at my first evening party.
You were tall and fair, just seventeen perhaps,
Talking to my two sisters. I kept silent
And never since have loved a tall fair girl,
Until last night in the small windy hours
When, floating up an unfamiliar staircase
And into someone's bedroom, there I found her
Posted beside the window in half-light
Wearing that same white dress with lacy sleeves.
She beckoned. I came closer. We embraced
Inseparably until the dream faded.
Her eyes shone clear and blue . . .

Who was it, though, impersonated you?

A Time of Waiting

The moment comes when my sound senses
Warn me to keep the pot at a quiet simmer,
Conclude no rash decisions, enter into
No random friendships, check the runaway tongue
And fix my mind in a close caul of doubt –
Which is more difficult, maybe, than to face
Night-long assaults of lurking furies.

The pool lies almost empty; I watch it nursed
By a thin stream. Such idle intervals
Are from waning moon to the new – a moon always
Holds the cords of my heart. Then patience, hands;
Dabble your nerveless fingers in the shallows;
A time shall come when she has need of them.

Dance of Words

To make them move, you should start from lightning
And not forecast the rhythm: rely on chance,
Or so-called chance for its bright emergence
Once lightning interpenetrates the dance.

Grant them their own traditional steps and postures
But see they dance it out again and again
Until only lightning is left to puzzle over –
The choreography plain, and the theme plain.

Notes

HERE LIVE YOUR LIFE OUT. Graves plays with a common fantasy or momentary feeling about the ideal place, a glimpse of which suggests that if only one lived there everything would be perfect. He reinforces it with specific details in the first section, but the second section is a gradual deflation: 'you could not alight', did not, and, even if you had, you know that events would have overtaken you. One of the characteristics of paradise is that it is always somewhere else and always impossible to reach. The poem is stitched together with casual and irregular rhymes until the full clinching rhyme at the end which satisfactorily brings the dream to a halt.

SURGICAL WARD: MEN. A poem about the power and strangeness of physical pain. Drugs, though we may mistrust them and may try to avoid them by being brave, can relieve it. Both pain ('A single white-hot eye') and its relief in a drug ('Lady Morphia') are personified.

A DREAM OF FRANCES SPEEDWELL. One of several poems by Graves about the tricks and recurrences of the past and memory. The recollection of the young girl from his own boyhood merges with what appears to be a recent happening in old age, a ghostly blurring of past and present. Yet though this coming together is mysterious, as usual in Graves the details are so precise that the picture becomes the more evocative because of its delicate particularity.

A TIME OF WAITING. Graves has described the theme of this poem as being 'a resolve not to prejudice the future by hasty action'. It is concerned with the *art* of patience, and can be read as a kind of memorandum, a comment on the precious weight of poetic responsibility. In his essay 'The Poet in a Valley of Dry Bones', originally delivered as a lecture when he was Oxford Professor of Poetry, Graves gives a characteristically idiosyncratic account of the poem's composition, and it is worth quoting at some length for the light it sheds on his practice (and somewhat mischievous self-dramatisation) as a poet. In an early draft, line 5 contained the phrase 'a close pattern of doubt'. Graves saw that *pattern* was too decorative a word and tried several alternatives including *frame* (too formal) and *net* ('a mind can hardly be fixed in a net'). Nothing satisfied him:

> Finding the exact word seemed of the greatest importance . . . . When I am writing prose and have a word on the tip of my tongue, or the nib of my pen, which somehow eludes me, I often consult Roget's *Thesaurus*. Reading the list of so-called synonyms in a word-group, I at once recognise the word I need. But I do not use Roget for poems. So, instead, on this occasion I went down to the sea, swam out to a small rocky island, and there the exact right word floated up to me from several fathoms down:
>
> > To take no rash decisions, enter into
> > No random friendships, check the run-away tongue
> > And fix my mind in a close caul of doubt.
>
> *Caul* surprised me, because I had not considered the word for at least twenty years; but later, reaching for the 'C' volume of the *O.E.D.*, I found that it held all the senses I needed. A caul is, first, a net cap confining the glory of a woman, her hair; then a gossamer web spun by spiders over grass, heavy with dew at dawn. Finally, it is the smooth, cap-like membrane with which a child is sometimes born, a lucky relic of his uterine experiences and, in English superstition, sovereign against death by drowning. A caul is thus the gentlest and happiest of all cerebral restraints . . . . That *close call* has a somewhat outmoded slang significance, was an accident that did not disturb me. The eye cannot mistake *caul* for *call*, and the eye commands the inner ear. Poetry is read, not listened to, nine times out of ten . . . . If a poem is lurking at the back of a poet's mind, and he has perfect confidence in bringing it to light under the trance, the key-words sooner or later will always fall into place. Or that is my own long-cherished superstition.

No mention is made of the change from 'To take' to 'Conclude' (line 3). Perhaps this might be discussed along similar lines.

DANCE OF WORDS. A poem, Graves is saying, occurs accidentally on purpose. The poet should attend to his own purpose as a craftsman and be grateful for the accident. Note how carefully, for example, Graves himself has attended to the word 'forecast' in the second line. He deploys it not only as part of the metaphor of spiritual atmospherics (weather forecast) but also in its basic sense of *casting beforehand*. This introduces a theme of fundamental concern to many poets: i.e. the dangers of too slavish an adherence to a preconceived metrical plan, composing (to use Ezra Pound's words) according to the metronome rather than the musical phrase. It is the difference between puppetry and choreography.

Stevie Smith

Stevie Smith was born in 1902. She spent most of her life living in the same house in an unfashionable part of north London, with an aunt who appears both in her own novel, *Novel on Yellow Paper* (1936) and in the play *Stevie* (later made into a film) by Hugh Whitemore. She died in 1971. She was a highly original and unclassifiable writer. Someone once said that she was like William Blake rewritten by Ogden Nash — a smart remark, but it does not really catch her unique mixture of whimsical gloom, eccentric commonsense, incantation, nursery rhyme, doggerel and rhythmical subtlety. The quality of her poems was underlined by her own readings (some of which were recorded and are available); sometimes she chanted or half sang them. Her *Collected Poems* were published in 1975.

Mrs Arbuthnot

Mrs Arbuthnot was a poet
A poet of high degree,
But her talent left her;
Now she lives at home by the sea.

In the morning she washes up,
In the afternoon she sleeps,
Only in the evenings sometimes
For her lost talent she weeps,

Crying: I should write a poem,
Can I look a wave in the face
If I do not write a poem about a sea-wave,
Putting the words in place.

Mrs Arbuthnot has died,
She has gone to heaven,
She is one with the heavenly combers now
And need not write about them.

Cry: She is a heavenly comber,
She runs with a comb of fire,
Nobody writes or wishes to
Who is one with their desire.

The Donkey

It was such a pretty little donkey
It had such pretty ears
And it used to gallop round the field so briskly
Though well down in years.

It was a retired donkey,
After a life-time of working
Between the shafts of regular employment
It was now free to go merrymaking.

Oh in its eyes was such a gleam
As is usually associated with youth
But it was not a youthful gleam really,
But full of mature truth.

And of the hilarity that goes with age,
As if to tell us sardonically
No hedged track lay before this donkey longer
But the sweet prairies of anarchy.

But the sweet prairies of anarchy
And the thought that keeps my heart up
That at last, in Death's odder anarchy,
Our pattern will be broken all up.
Though precious we are momentarily, donkey,
I aspire to be broken up.

Black March

I have a friend
At the end
Of the world.
His name is a breath

Of fresh air.
He is dressed in

Grey chiffon. At least
I think it is chiffon.
It has a
Peculiar look, like smoke.

It wraps him round
It blows out of place
It conceals him
I have not seen his face.

But I have seen his eyes, they are
As pretty and bright
As raindrops on black twigs
In March, and heard him say:

I am a breath
Of fresh air for you, a change
By and by.

Black March I call him
Because of his eyes
Being like March raindrops
On black twigs.

(Such a pretty time when the sky
Behind black twigs can be seen
Stretched out in one
Uninterrupted
Cambridge blue as cold as snow.)

But this friend
Whatever new names I give him
Is an old friend. He says:

Whatever names you give me
I am
A breath of fresh air,
A change for you.

11

Tenuous and Precarious

Tenuous and Precarious
Were my guardians,
Precarious and Tenuous,
Two Romans.

My father was Hazardous,
Hazardous,
Dear old man,
Three Romans.

There was my brother Spurious,
Spurious Posthumous,
Spurious was spurious
Was four Romans.

My husband was Perfidious,
He was perfidious,
Five Romans.

Surreptitious, our son,
Was surreptitious,
He was six Romans.

Our cat Tedious
Still lives,
Count not Tedious
Yet.

My name is Finis,
Finis, Finis,
I am Finis,
Six, five, four, three, two,
One Roman,
Finis.

Not Waving but Drowning

Nobody heard him, the dead man,
But still he lay moaning:
I was much further out than you thought
And not waving but drowning.

Poor chap, he always loved larking
And now he's dead
It must have been too cold for him his heart gave way,
They said.

Oh, no no no, it was too cold always
(Still the dead one lay moaning)
I was much too far out all my life
And not waving but drowning.

Notes

MRS ARBUTHNOT. Some of Stevie Smith's funniest and most poignant poems are about the failure of inspiration, about poets who feel they have failed or have not been appreciated enough, and about the resentment poets sometimes feel at the thought that misery produces poems while happiness does not. Compare, for example, 'Thoughts about the Person from Porlock' and 'The Poet Hin' in the *Collected Poems*.

THE DONKEY and BLACK MARCH. As in 'Black March' and many other poems, Stevie Smith in 'The Donkey' writes as one who, like Keats — though she would never have expressed herself in such a way — was 'half in love with easeful death'. The jaunty irregular metre, the casual rhymes, have a flavour which is partly naive, partly knowing. 'The hilarity that goes with age' was one side of her spirit, the gently melancholy acceptance of 'Black March' another.

TENUOUS AND PRECARIOUS. Playing with English adjectives of Latin derivation, she creates a comic, sly, doom-laden family of Romans. As usual the conclusion is Death, and so is the speaker.

NOT WAVING BUT DROWNING. This is possibly Stevie Smith's best known poem, and the title phrase could be said to have entered our language. The gossipy tone of the second stanza only serves to heighten the tragic sense of desolation caught so memorably in the figure of the distant, waving man who is signalling neither Hello nor Goodbye but Help!

John Betjeman

John Betjeman was born in 1906 and has been Poet Laureate since 1972. When the first version of his *Collected Poems* was published in 1958, the book was an immediate popular success, perhaps partly for non-poetic reasons; he has been a frequent and memorable broadcaster and television personality, putting much genial energy into the championing of Victorian architecture and Victorian verse, antiquarian preservationism and the presentation of his other special enthusiasms. But both W. H. Auden and Philip Larkin have praised him highly, Auden for his versatile technical skill, Larkin for the 'dramatic urgency' that springs from 'what he really feels about real life'. It is true that his most frequently quoted poems are those, such as 'A Subaltern's Love-song' ('Miss Joan Hunter Dunn, Miss Joan Hunter Dunn'), which are gently absurd essays in light verse, making fun of certain English attitudes, while at the same time appearing to share so many of those attitudes that the poet's own stance is sometimes a little uncertain. But there is an altogether more astringent side to Betjeman, in which nostalgia, fear, hard-won faith and simple goodness contend, and a basic melancholy.

NW5 & N6

Red cliffs arise. And up them service lifts
Soar with the groceries to silver heights.
Lissenden Mansions. And my memory sifts
Lilies from lily-like electric lights
And Irish stew smells from the smell of prams
And roar of seas from roar of London trams.

Out of it all my memory carves the quiet
Of that dark privet hedge where pleasures breed,
There first, intent upon its leafy diet,
I watched the looping caterpillar feed
And saw it hanging in a gummy froth
Till, weeks on, from the chrysalis burst the moth.

I see black oak twigs outlined on the sky,
Red squirrels on the Burdett-Coutts estate.
I ask my nurse the question 'Will I die?'
As bells from sad St Anne's ring out so late,
'And if I do die, will I go to Heaven?'
Highgate at eventide. Nineteen-eleven.

'You will. I won't.' From that cheap nursery-maid,
Sadist and puritan as now I see,
I first learned what it was to be afraid,
Forcibly fed when sprawled across her knee
Lock'd into cupboards, left alone all day,
'World without end.' What fearsome words to pray.

'World without end.' It was not what she'ld do
That frightened me so much as did her fear
And guilt at endlessness. I caught them too,
Hating to think of sphere succeeding sphere
Into eternity and God's dread will
I caught her terror then. I have it still.

From Summoned by Bells

For myself,
I knew as soon as I could read and write
That I must be a poet. Even today,
When all the way from Cambridge comes a wind
To blow the lamps out every time they're lit,
I know that I must light mine up again.

My first attraction was to tripping lines;
Internal rhyming, as in Shelley's 'Cloud',
Seemed then perfection. 'O'er' and 'ere' and 'e'en'
Were words I liked to use. My father smiled:
'And how's our budding bard? Let what you write
Be funny, John, and be original.'
Secretly proud, I showed off merrily.
But certain as the stars above the twigs
And deeply fearful as the pealing bells
And everlasting as the racing surf
Blown back upon itself in Polzeath Bay,
My urge was to encase in rhythm and rhyme
The things I saw and felt (I could not *think*).

And so, at sunset, off to Hampstead Heath
I went with pencil and with writing-pad
And stood tip-toe upon a little hill,
Awaiting inspiration from the sky.
'Look! there's a poet!', people might exclaim
On footpaths near. The muse inspired my pen:
The sunset tipped with gold St Michael's church,
Shouts of boys bathing came from Highgate Ponds,
The elms that hid the houses of the great
Rustled with mystery, and dirt-grey sheep
Grazed in the foreground; but the lines of verse
Came out like parodies of *A & M*.

The gap between my feelings and my skill
Was so immense, I wonder I went on.
A stretch of heather seen at Haslemere
And 'Up the airy mountain' (Allingham)
Merged in the magic of my Highgate pen:

When the moors are pink with heather
  When the sky's as blue as the sea,
Marching all together
  Come fairy folk so wee.

My goodness me! It seemed perfection then –
The brilliance of the rhymes A B, A B!
The vastness and the daintiness combined!
The second verse was rather less inspired:

  Some in green and some in red
    And some with a violet plume,
  And a little cap on each tiny head
    Watching the bright white moon.

I copied out the lines into a book,
A leather-bound one given me for verse
And stamped with my initials. There it stood
On the first page, that poem – a reproach.
In later years I falsified the date
To make it seem that I was only seven,
Not eight, when these weak stanzas were composed . . . .

. . . . Atlantic rollers bursting in my ears,
And pealing church-bells and the puff of trains,
The sight of sailing clouds, the smell of grass –
Were always calling out to me for words.
I caught at them and missed and missed again.
'Catch hold,' my father said, 'catch hold like this!',
Trying to teach me how to carpenter,
'Not *that* way, boy! When will you ever learn?' –
I dug the chisel deep into my hand.
'Shoot!' said my father, helping with my gun
And aiming at the rabbit – 'Quick, boy, fire!'
But I had not released the safety-catch.
I was a poet. That was why I failed.
My faith in this chimera brought an end
To all my father's hopes. In later years,
Now old and ill, he asked me once again

18

To carry on the firm, I still refused.
And now when I behold, fresh-published, new,
A further volume of my verse, I see
His kind grey eyes look woundedly at mine,
I see his workmen seeking other jobs,
And that red granite obelisk that marks
The family grave in Highgate Cemetery
Points an accusing finger to the sky.

Executive

I am a young executive. No cuffs than mine are cleaner;
I have a Slimline brief-case and I use the firm's Cortina.
In every roadside hostelry from here to Burgess Hill
The *maîtres d'hôtel* all know me well and let me sign the bill.

You ask me what it is I do. Well actually, you know,
I'm partly a liaison man and partly P.R.O.
Essentially I integrate the current export drive
And basically I'm viable from ten o'clock till five.

For vital off-the-record work – that's talking transport-wise –
I've a scarlet Aston-Martin – and does she go? She flies!
Pedestrians and dogs and cats – we mark them down for
    slaughter.
I also own a speed-boat which has never touched the water.

She's built of fibre-glass, of course. I call her 'Mandy Jane'
After a bird I used to know – No soda, please, just plain –
And how did I acquire her? Well to tell you about that
And to put you in the picture I must wear my other hat.

I do some mild developing. The sort of place I need
Is a quiet country market town that's rather run to seed.
A luncheon and a drink or two, a little *savoir faire* –
I fix the Planning Officer, the Town Clerk and the Mayor.

And if some preservationist attempts to interfere
A 'dangerous structure' notice from the Borough Engineer
Will settle any buildings that are standing in our way –
The modern style, sir, with respect, has really come to stay.

Notes

NW5 & N6. Betjeman's childhood in Highgate in north London is looked at more fully in his verse autobiography, *Summoned by Bells*, from which an extract is included here. The oppressive weight of the sense of sin in childhood, and the loss of innocence, can also be found in several short Betjeman poems, such as 'Norfolk' and 'Original Sin on the Sussex Coast'. As usual in Betjeman, much of the force of 'NW5 & N6' comes from the precisely remembered details and the naming of names. In 1911 he was five years old.

From SUMMONED BY BELLS. Most of *Summoned by Bells* is written in regular but casual blank verse, interspersed with shorter lyrical pieces. These sections look with affectionate amusement at his first childhood efforts to write poetry. Polzeath Bay is in Cornwall, where Betjeman spent many childhood holidays. *A & M* is *Hymns Ancient and Modern*, one of the two chief Anglican hymnbooks. William Allingham was a minor nineteenth-century poet.

EXECUTIVE. A breezy self-portrait of a typical Betjeman villain, full of ruthlessness, brash insensitivity, and jargon ('viable', 'off-the-record', 'transport-wise', 'to put you in the picture I must wear my other hat'). The 'developer' who causes 'a quiet country market town that's rather run to seed' to be torn to pieces in the interests of supposed modernisation is opposed to the 'pre-servationist', such as Betjeman himself, who has done a great deal to give English people a conscience and sense of responsibility about their recent as well as their remote past.

W. H. Auden

W. H. Auden was born in 1907. In his early twenties he was recognised as the finest poet of his generation, and perhaps the finest poet since T. S. Eliot. In the 1930s he was associated in the public mind with other poets of the supposed 'Left' – Stephen Spender, C. Day Lewis, Louis MacNeice – though in fact not much of Auden's work is directly political. What is most striking about it is that it is so various, and went on being various and unpredictable until his death. Some people say that there was a falling-off in the quality of his poems after his departure for the United States in January 1939 (later he became an American citizen), and it is true that a number of them in the 1940s and afterwards lack the peculiarly urgent, warning force of what he was writing in the 1930s. But he never ceased to be an exuberant, inventive, technically audacious writer, fertile with ideas and phrases. Readers of his postwar poems (and we have included nothing earlier than our starting date of 1945) should be prepared to consult, now and then, what Auden – in 'The Cave of Making', included here – called 'dictionaries (the very best money can buy)'. At the same time, he could be direct, colloquial, biting, as in 'August, 1968'. The sheer quantity of Auden's work – in verse, prose and drama – is immense. For a copious view of what he was up to before the war, the best single volume is *The English Auden: poems, essays, and dramatic writings, 1927–1939* (1977). There is also a *Collected Poems*, but this does not yet include some of the more recent volumes, the most important of which are *About the House* (1966), *City Without Walls* (1969), and *Epistle to a Godson* (1972). Auden died in Vienna in 1973.

The Cave of Making

(*In Memoriam Louis MacNeice*)

For this and for all enclosures like it the archetype
    is Weland's Stithy, an antre
more private than a bedroom even, for neither lovers nor
    maids are welcome, but without a
bedroom's secrets: from the Olivetti portable,
    the dictionaries (the very
best money can buy), the heaps of paper, it is evident
    what must go on. Devoid of
flowers and family photographs, all is subordinate
    here to a function, designed to
discourage daydreams – hence windows averted from plausible
    videnda but admitting a light one
could mend a watch by – and to sharpen hearing: reached by an
    outside staircase, domestic
noises and odours, the vast background of natural
    life are shut off. Here silence
is turned into objects.
    I wish, Louis, I could have shown it you
    while you were still in public,
and the house and garden: lover of women and Donegal,
    from your perspective you'd notice
sights I overlook, and in turn take a scholar's interest
    in facts I could tell you (for instance,
four miles to our east, at a wood palisade, Carolingian
    Bavaria stopped, beyond it
unknowable nomads). Friends we became by personal
    choice, but fate had already
made us neighbours. For Grammar we both inherited
    good mongrel barbarian English
which never completely succumbed to the Roman rhetoric
    or the Roman gravity, that nonsense
which stood none. Though neither of our dads, like Horace's,
    wiped his nose on his forearm,
neither was porphyry-born, and our ancestors probably
    were among those plentiful subjects

it cost less money to murder. Born so, both of us
 became self-conscious at a moment
when locomotives were named after knights in Malory,
 Science to schoolboys was known as
Stinks, and the Manor still was politically numinous:
 both watched with mixed feelings
the sack of Silence, the churches empty, the cavalry
 go, the Cosmic Model
become German, and any faith if we had it, in immanent
 virtue died. More than ever
life-out-there is goodly, miraculous, lovable,
 but we shan't, not since Stalin and Hitler,
trust ourselves ever again: we know that, subjectively,
 all is possible.
  To you, though,
ever since, last Fall, you quietly slipped out of Granusion,
 our moist garden, into
the Country of Unconcern, no possibility
 matters. I wish you hadn't
caught that cold, but the dead we miss are easier
 to talk to: with those no longer
tensed by problems one cannot feel shy and, anyway,
 when playing cards or drinking
or pulling faces are out of the question, what else is there
 to do but talk to the voices
of conscience they have become? From now on, as a visitor
 who needn't be met at the station,
your influence is welcome at any hour in my ubity,
 especially here, where titles
from *Poems* to *The Burning Perch* offer proof positive
 of the maker you were, with whom I
once collaborated, once at a weird Symposium
 exchanged winks as a juggins
went on about Alienation.
Who would, for preference,
 be a bard in an oral culture,
obliged at drunken feasts to improvise a eulogy
 of some beefy illiterate burner,

giver of rings, or depend for bread on the moods of a
    Baroque Prince, expected,
like his dwarf, to amuse? After all, it's rather a privilege
    amid the affluent traffic
to serve this unpopular art which cannot be turned into
    background noise for study
or hung as a status trophy by rising executives,
    cannot be 'done' like Venice
or abridged like Tolstoy, but stubbornly still insists upon
    being read or ignored: our handful
of clients at least can rune. (It's heartless to forget about
    the underdeveloped countries,
but a starving ear is as deaf as a suburban optimist's:
    to stomachs only the Hindu
integers truthfully speak.) Our forerunners might envy us
    our remnant still able to listen:
as Nietzsche said they would, the *plebs* have got steadily
    denser, the *optimates*
quicker still on the uptake. (Today, even Talleyrand
    might seem a naïf: he had so
little to cope with.) I should like to become, if possible,
    a minor atlantic Goethe,
with his passion for weather and stones but without his silliness
    re the Cross: at times a bore, but,
while knowing Speech can at best, a shadow echoing
    the silent light, bear witness
to the Truth it is not, he wished it were, as the Francophile
    gaggle of pure songsters
are too vain to. We're not musicians: to stink of Poetry
    is unbecoming, and never
to be dull shows a lack of taste. Even a limerick
    ought to be something a man of
honour, awaiting death from cancer or a firing squad,
    could read without contempt: (at
that frontier I wouldn't dare speak to anyone
    in either a prophet's bellow
or a diplomat's whisper).
Seeing you know our mystery

from the inside and therefore
how much, in our lonely dens, we need the companionship
    of our good dead, to give us
comfort on dowly days when the self is a nonentity
    dumped on a mound of nothing,
to break the spell of our self-enchantment when lip-smacking
    imps of mawk and hooey
write with us what they will, you won't think me imposing if
    I ask you to stay at my elbow
until cocktail time: dear Shade, for your elegy
    I should have been able to manage
something more like you than this egocentric monologue,
    but accept it for friendship's sake.

The Fall of Rome

The piers are pummelled by the waves;
In a lonely field the rain
Lashes an abandoned train;
Outlaws fill the mountain caves.

Fantastic grow the evening gowns;
Agents of the Fisc pursue
Absconding tax-defaulters through
The sewers of provincial towns.

Private rites of magic send
The temple prostitutes to sleep;
All the literati keep
An imaginary friend.

Cerebrotonic Cato may
Extol the Ancient Disciplines,
But the muscle-bound Marines
Mutiny for food and pay.

Caesar's double-bed is warm
As an unimportant clerk
Writes I DO NOT LIKE MY WORK
On a pink official form.

Unendowed with wealth or pity,
Little birds with scarlet legs,
Sitting on their speckled eggs,
Eye each flu-infected city.

Altogether elsewhere, vast
Herds of reindeer move across
Miles and miles of golden moss,
Silently and very fast.

The Shield of Achilles

  She looked over his shoulder
   For vines and olive trees,
  Marble well-governed cities
   And ships upon untamed seas,
  But there on the shining metal
   His hands had put instead
  An artificial wilderness
   And a sky like lead.

A plain without a feature, bare and brown,
 No blade of grass, no sign of neighbourhood,
Nothing to eat and nowhere to sit down,
 Yet, congregated on its blankness, stood
 An unintelligible multitude.
A million eyes, a million boots in line,
Without expression, waiting for a sign.

Out of the air a voice without a face
    Proved by statistics that some cause was just
In tones as dry and level as the place:
    No one was cheered and nothing was discussed;
    Column by column in a cloud of dust
They marched away enduring a belief
Whose logic brought them, somewhere else, to grief.

                She looked over his shoulder
                    For ritual pieties,
                White flower-garlanded heifers,
                    Libation and sacrifice,
                But there on the shining metal
                    Where the altar should have been,
                She saw by his flickering forge-light
                    Quite another scene.

Barbed wire enclosed an arbitrary spot
    Where bored officials lounged (one cracked a joke)
And sentries sweated for the day was hot:
    A crowd of ordinary decent folk
    Watched from without and neither moved nor spoke
As three pale figures were led forth and bound
To three posts driven upright in the ground.

The mass and majesty of this world, all
    That carries weight and always weighs the same
Lay in the hands of others; they were small
    And could not hope for help and no help came:
    What their foes liked to do was done, their shame
Was all the worst could wish; they lost their pride
And died as men before their bodies died.

She looked over his shoulder
    For athletes at their games,
Men and women in a dance
    Moving their sweet limbs
Quick, quick, to music,
    But there on the shining shield
His hands had set no dancing-floor
    But a weed-choked field

A ragged urchin, aimless and alone,
    Loitered about that vacancy, a bird
Flew up to safety from his well-aimed stone:
    That girls are raped, that two boys knife a third,
Were axioms to him, who'd never heard
Of any world where promises were kept,
Or one could weep because another wept.

    The thin-lipped armourer,
        Hephaestos hobbled away,
    Thetis of the shining breasts
        Cried out in dismay
    At what the god had wrought
        To please her son, the strong
    Iron-hearted man-slaying Achilles
        Who would not live long.

August, 1968

The Ogre does what ogres can,
Deeds quite impossible for Man,
But one prize is beyond his reach,
The Ogre cannot master Speech:
About a subjugated plain,
Among its desperate and slain,
The Ogre stalks with hands on hips,
While drivel gushes from his lips.

In Due Season

Spring-time, Summer and Fall: days to behold a world
Antecedent to our knowing, where flowers think
Theirs concretely in scent-colours and beasts, the same
Age all over, pursue dumb horizontal lives
On one level of conduct and so cannot be
Secretary to man's plot to become divine.

Lodged in all is a set metronome: thus, in May
Bird-babes still in the egg click to each other *Hatch!*;
June-struck cuckoos go off-pitch; when obese July
Turns earth's heating up, unknotting their poisoned ropes,
Vipers move into play; warned by October's nip,
Younger leaves to the old give the releasing draught.

Winter, though, has the right tense for a look indoors
At ourselves, and with First Names to sit face-to-face,
Time for reading of thoughts, time for the trying-out
Of new metres and new recipes, proper time
To reflect on events noted in warmer months
Till, transmuted they take part in a human tale.

There, responding to our cry for intelligence,
Nature's mask is relaxed into a mobile grin,
Stones, old shoes, come alive, born sacramental signs,
Nod to us in the First Person of mysteries
They know nothing about, bearing a message from
The invisible sole Source of specific things.

Talking to Myself
(for Oliver Sacks)

Spring this year in Austria started off benign,
the heavens lucid, the air stable, the about
sane to all feeders, vegetate or bestial:
the deathless minerals looked pleased with their regime,
where what is not forbidden is compulsory.

Shadows of course there are, Porn-Ads, with-it clergy,
and hubby next door has taken to the bottle,
but You have preserved Your poise, strange rustic object,
whom I, made in God's Image but already warped,
a malapert will-worship, must bow to as Me.

My mortal manor, the carnal territory
allotted to my manage, my fosterling too,
I must earn cash to support, my tutor also,
but for whose neural instructions I could never
acknowledge what is or imagine what is not.

Instinctively passive, I guess, having neither
fangs nor talons nor hooves nor venom, and therefore
too prone to let the sun go down upon Your funk,
a poor smeller, or rather a censor of smells,
with an omnivore palate that can take hot food.

Unpredictably, decades ago, You arrived
among that unending cascade of creatures spewed
from Nature's maw. A random event, says Science.
Random my bottom! A true miracle, say I,
for who is not certain that he was meant to be?

As You augmented and developed a profile,
I looked at Your looks askance. *His architecture*
should have been much more imposing: I've been let down!
By now, though, I've gotten used to Your proportions
and, all things considered, I might have fared far worse.

Seldom have You been a bother. For many years
You were, I admit, a martyr to horn-colic
(it did no good to tell You – *But I'm not in love!*):
how stoutly, though, You've repelled all germ invasions,
but never chastised my tantrums with a megrim.

You are the Injured Party for, if short-sighted,
I am the book-worm who tired You, if short-winded
as cigarette addicts are, I was the pusher
who got You hooked. (Had we been both a bit younger,
I might well have mischiefed You worse with a needle.)

I'm always amazed at how little I know You.
Your coasts and outgates I know, for I govern there,
but what goes on inland, the rites, the social codes,
Your torrents, salt and sunless, remain enigmas:
what I believe is on doctors' hearsay only.

Our marriage is a drama, but no stage-play where
what is not spoken is not thought: in our theatre
all that I cannot syllable You will pronounce
in acts whose *raison d'être* escapes me. Why secrete
fluid when I dole, or stretch Your lips when I joy?

Demands to close or open, include or eject,
must come from Your corner, are no province of mine
(all I have done is to provide the time-table
of hours when You may put them): but what is Your work
when I librate between a glum and a frolic?

For dreams I, quite irrationally, reproach You.
All I know is that I don't choose them: if I could,
they would conform to some prosodic discipline,
mean just what they say. Whatever point nocturnal
manias make, as a poet I disapprove.

Thanks to Your otherness, Your jocular concords,
so unlike my realm of dissonance and anger,
You can serve me as my emblem for the Cosmos:
for human congregations, though, as Hobbes perceived
the apposite sign is some ungainly monster.

Whoever coined the phrase *The Body Politic*?
All States we've lived in, or historians tell of,
have had shocking health, psychosomatic cases,
physicked by sadists or glozing expensive quacks:
when I read the papers, You seem an Adonis.

Time, we both know, will decay You, and already
I'm scared of our divorce: I've seen some horrid ones.
Remember: when *Le bon Dieu* says to You *Leave him!*,
please, please, for His sake and mine, pay no attention
to my piteous *Don'ts*, but bugger off quickly.

Notes

THE CAVE OF MAKING. This is one of twelve poems in a sequence called 'Thanksgiving for a Habitat', each of which looks at a different room in Auden's house in Austria, from cellar to attic. In 'The Cave of Making' we are in the study, where the poet writes; and, appropriately, the poem is dedicated to the memory of Auden's fellow poet and friend from undergraduate days at Oxford, Louis MacNeice, who had recently died.

The privacy of this room is stressed – a place of silence and concentration, without the distractions of 'natural life'. But the poem quickly turns from consideration of the room and its function to the common background shared by Auden and Mac-Neice: the same age and the same class (Auden's father was a senior doctor, MacNeice's a senior clergyman) gave them in many ways a common vantage point. From there it becomes a meditation on the advantages poetry has – and particularly the poet today – over other arts and periods, because it has nothing to do with status and is in fact an 'unpopular art'. On this the integrity of the poet must rely.

The poem's discursiveness – part elegy, part meditation, part 'egocentric monologue' – is typical of much of Auden's later work. So is the use of rare words: 'antre', 'videnda', 'mawk and hooey' – and the bold personalising of abstractions ('the Country of Unconcern' = death, 'the sack of Silence' probably means the noisy invasion of privacy by modern propaganda-dispensing media).

THE FALL OF ROME. The neat biting quatrains of this poem effectively give a picture of a mysteriously declining civilisation, which shares some features with the decadence of ancient Rome but has others which are modern (a train, 'a pink official form'). Part of the force comes from the apparently arbitrary juxtaposition of human (or social) details with ones which, though 'natural', are sinister – such as the birds looking at 'each flu-infected city', and the reindeer in the final stanza: both are indifferent to the fate of a collapsing culture.

THE SHIELD OF ACHILLES. The mythological background is that, in Homer's *Iliad* (Book 18), Hephaestos, the god of fire and armourer to the gods – the Greek equivalent of the Roman Vulcan – makes a magnificent shield for Achilles, along with the rest of Achilles' armour. This shield has the power of reflecting, or foretelling, the future, and in the poem Auden alternates short-lined stanzas concerned with the Homeric story with more solid stanzas in iambic pentameter which look at scenes of brutality and violence which are more specifically twentieth-century. The future is foreseen in the past. At the heart of the poem, in the fifth and sixth stanzas, the scene is a (or the) crucifixion which at the same time carries modern characteristics, in particular the barbed wire, which summons up thoughts of concentration camps.

AUGUST, 1968. The month during which the Soviet Union sent troops into Czechoslovakia to overturn the 'liberal' communist regime of Dubček, after the so-called 'Prague Spring'. This epigram can be compared with much earlier ones by Auden, such as 'Epitaph on a Tyrant', written in January 1939:

> Perfection, of a kind, was what he was after,
> And the poetry he invented was easy to understand;
> He knew human folly like the back of his hand,
> And was greatly interested in armies and fleets;
> When he laughed, respectable senators burst with laughter,
> And when he cried the little children died in the streets.

IN DUE SEASON. A poem which contrasts the vivid but set routine of Nature with the mysterious patterns of human invention, the 'set metronome' (line 7) with the 'mobile grin' (line 20). As in so much of Auden's later work, the vocabulary is wittily reductive (e.g. 'when obese July/Turns earth's heating up') but the argument it serves is a profound one: it is a poetic method which exemplifies Auden's fundamental view of man as *homo ludens* and of poetry as a serious game.

TALKING TO MYSELF. There is a tradition, in verse, of abstract dialogues between the Soul and the Body but here, in a monologue, the ageing Auden addresses his own body with an engaging intimacy and candour. The tone *librates* (a handy *OED* is necessary when reading the later Auden) between *glum* and *frolic* – a blend of stoicism, pathos and good humour. The poem is dedicated to the poet's friend Oliver Sacks, a doctor whose experiments in the release of 'sleeping-sickness' patients through use of the miracle drug L-DOPA greatly fascinated Auden. Sacks's moving book of case studies, *Awakenings*, concerned as it is with the relation of personality and body, might be read as a companion to 'Talking to Myself'. It was published in 1973, the year of Auden's death.

Louis MacNeice

Louis MacNeice was born in 1907. For several years he was a university lecturer in classics, but for a much longer period — over twenty years — he worked for the BBC as a radio writer and producer. When he died in 1963 it was generally agreed that his recent poems were as good as any during his long writing career; but gradually his reputation has increased beyond that, so that now he is often referred to as being not only Auden's most important follower but as being of almost equal stature. He came from a strict Protestant background in Northern Ireland, though at an early age he was sent to boarding school in England. A mingled nostalgia for and fear of his childhood appears again and again in his poems, together with a sense of rootlessness, a delight in ordinary things (food, drink, games), and a sort of melancholy or wistful playfulness. His *Collected Poems* were published in 1966.

Apple Blossom

The first blossom was the best blossom
For the child who never had seen an orchard;
For the youth whom whisky had led astray
The morning after was the first day.

The first apple was the best apple
For Adam before he heard the sentence;
When the flaming sword endorsed the Fall
The trees were his to plant for all.

The first ocean was the best ocean
For the child from streets of doubt and litter;
For the youth for whom the skies unfurled
His first love was his first world.

But the first verdict seemed the worst verdict
When Adam and Eve were expelled from Eden;
Yet when the bitter gates clanged to
The sky beyond was just as blue.

For the next ocean is the first ocean
And the last ocean is the first ocean
And, however often the sun may rise,
A new thing dawns upon our eyes.

For the last blossom is the first blossom
And the first blossom is the best blossom
And when from Eden we take our way
The morning after is the first day.

The Slow Starter

A watched clock never moves, they said:
Leave it alone and you'll grow up.
Nor will the sulking holiday train
Start sooner if you stamp your feet.
  He left the clock to go its way;
  The whistle blew, the train went gay.

Do not press me so, she said;
Leave me alone and I will write
But not just yet, I am sure you know
The problem. Do not count the days.
  He left the calendar alone;
  The postman knocked, no letter came.

O never force the pace, they said;
Leave it alone, you have lots of time,
Your kind of work is none the worse
For slow maturing. Do not rush.
  He took their tip, he took his time,
  And found his time and talent gone.

Oh you have had your chance, It said;
Left it alone and it was one.
Who said a watched clock never moves?
Look at it now. Your chance was I.
  He turned and saw the accusing clock
  Race like a torrent round a rock.

Old Masters Abroad

Painfully grinning faces like dogs' or
Inattentive like cats' all over
The static globe affect to be lectured
By the singing birds of unknown England.

Shakespeare flaunts his codpiece at dhoti,
Ditto at sari, Pope with his clouded
Cane conducts the dancers of Bali,
The lesser celandine sprouts in Lagos.

And the skylark crying 'Bird I never!'
Routs parrakeet, hornbill, kookaburra,
While the nightingale puts on spurs in Hampstead
To rip the guts from the decadent bulbul.

Wee sleekit courin' timorous warthog!
Tirra lirra by Kabul River!
The elmtree bole is in tiny leaf but
Not for long because of the termites.

At Bablockhythe the stripling Ganges
Burns on her ghats the scholar gypsy,
There's a deathly hush on the rocks of Aden,
Nine bean rows rise in the Kalahari.

The faces listen or not. The lecturers
Mop their memories. All over the static
Globe the needle sticks in the groove.
It is overtime now for the Old Masters.

Soap Suds

This brand of soap has the same smell as once in the big
House he visited when he was eight: the walls of the bathroom
     open
To reveal a lawn where a great yellow ball rolls back through a
     hoop
To rest at the head of a mallet held in the hands of a child.

And these were the joys of that house: a tower with a telescope;
Two great faded globes, one of the earth, one of the stars;
A stuffed black dog in the hall; a walled garden with bees;
A rabbit warren; a rockery; a vine under glass; the sea.

To which he has now returned. The day of course is fine
And a grown-up voice cries Play! The mallet slowly swings,
Then crack, a great gong booms from the dog-dark hall and the
     ball
Skims forward through the hoop and then through the next and
     then

Through hoops where no hoops were and each dissolves in turn
And the grass has grown head-high and an angry voice cries
     Play!
But the ball is lost and the mallet slipped long since from the
     hands
Under the running tap that are not the hands of a child.

The Truisms

His father gave him a box of truisms
Shaped like a coffin, then his father died;
The truisms remained on the mantelpiece
As wooden as the playbox they had been packed in
Or that other his father skulked inside.

Then he left home, left the truisms behind him
Still on the mantelpiece, met love, met war,
Sordor, disappointment, defeat, betrayal,
Till through disbeliefs he arrived at a house
He could not remember seeing before,

And he walked straight in; it was where he had come from
And something told him the way to behave.
He raised his hand and blessed his home;
The truisms flew and perched on his shoulders
And a tall tree sprouted from his father's grave.

Thalassa

Run out the boat, my broken comrades;
Let the old seaweed crack, the surge
Burgeon oblivious of the last
Embarkation of feckless men,
Let every adverse force converge –
Here we must needs embark again.

Run up the sail, my heartsick comrades;
Let each horizon tilt and lurch –
You know the worst: your wills are fickle,
Your values blurred, your hearts impure
And your past life a ruined church –
But let your poison be your cure.

Put out to sea, ignoble comrades,
Whose record shall be noble yet;
Butting through scarps of moving marble
The narwhal dares us to be free;
By a high star our course is set,
Our end is Life. Put out to sea.

Notes

APPLE BLOSSOM. This is typical of a number of MacNeice's later poems, which have a very marked lyrical movement, often like traditional songs or nursery rhymes. The notion of childhood as a lost Eden is common in MacNeice, but sometimes alleviated, as in this poem, by the jaunty suggestion that even after the expulsion from the Garden new things suggest themselves.

THE SLOW STARTER. A kind of reverse image to 'Apple Blossom', in which the pessimism and melancholy are uppermost, but again using a simple song-like measure.

OLD MASTERS ABROAD. In the intervals of working as a writer/producer for the BBC Features Department, MacNeice did a good deal of lecturing abroad for the British Council and other bodies. In this poem he comically plays with the incongruities of teaching famous British poems in exotic places. 'A nest of singing birds' is how Dr Johnson described Pembroke College, Oxford, in his own day. Most of the flora, fauna and places MacNeice refers to come from Romantic poems: Wordsworth's lesser celandine, Shelley's skylark, Keats's nightingale, a warthog instead of Burns's mouse ('Wee sleekit courin' timorous . . .'), Browning's elmtree bole, Matthew Arnold's Bablockhythe and scholar gypsy, Newbolt's 'There's a deathly hush in the Close tonight', Yeats's nine bean rows.

SOAP SUDS. Like 'Apple Blossom', but more circumstantially and more darkly, this is a recreation of childhood. The sense of smell is often the most powerful sense in bringing back a moment of the past, as here, where the smell of a particular soap conjures up a whole world of remote memory. The scene is probably from his boyhood in Ulster, though this 'big house' is not mentioned in MacNeice's autobiography *The Strings Are False*.

THE TRUISMS. The 'father' in this poem is not necessarily or primarily MacNeice's own; but it is true that John Frederick MacNeice, who was a Protestant clergyman (and later a bishop) in Northern Ireland, was someone of whom the poet was in awe. Louis MacNeice felt that, unlike his father, he would not have with him on judgement day any 'responsibly compiled/Account books of a devout, precise routine'. (The quotation comes from a poem called 'The Strand'.) A truism is by definition an obvious truth, so obvious and trivial that it hardly needs to be mentioned. How does this square with the 'disbeliefs' in the second stanza, or the images of inheritance and growth in the last stanza? Do we inevitably inherit the 'truisms' we grow up with?

THALASSA. This may be the last poem MacNeice wrote: it was found among his manuscripts after his death. The title is the Greek word for the sea. Clearly the poem is meant to echo the story of Ulysses, and perhaps specifically to be a variant on Tennyson's poem 'Ulysses', in its hopeless acceptance of hope. The structure is simple, but the patterning of syntax and internal rhyme ('surge/Burgeon', 'marble . . . narwhal') shows MacNeice's craftsmanship as clearly marked at his end as in his earlier poems.

Roy Fuller

Roy Fuller was born in 1912. For the whole of his working life outside his writing he was a solicitor until his retirement, and he has rather ruefully referred to his career as 'part managerial, part poetic'. That rueful tone is typical of one side of Roy Fuller's poetry, a tacit acceptance that he is making the best of a bad job. But in fact he is also an unashamedly intellectual poet of an adventurous sort, drawing on a wide range of reading and speculation about history, science, music and much else (see the note to 'Autobiography of a Lungworm'). He has said that one criterion of success in poetry is 'brain power allied at least to a dogged alertness and integrity', and that characterises very well his own virtues. He published a volume of *Collected Poems* in 1962. Since then he has published several more individual books, including *New Poems* (1968), *Tiny Tears* (1973), and *From the Joke Shop* (1975).

Translation

Now that the barbarians have got as far as Picra,
And all the new music is written in the twelve-tone scale,
And I am anyway approaching my fortieth birthday,
    I will dissemble no longer.

I will stop expressing my belief in the rosy
Future of man, and accept the evidence
Of a couple of wretched wars and innumerable
    Abortive revolutions.

I will cease to blame the stupidity of the slaves
Upon their masters and nurture, and will say,
Plainly, that they are enemies to culture,
    Advancement and cleanliness.

From progressive organisations, from quarterlies
Devoted to daring verse, from membership of
Committees, from letters of various protest
    I shall withdraw forthwith.

When they call me reactionary I shall smile,
Secure in another dimension. When they say
'Cinna has ceased to matter' I shall know
    How well I reflect the times.

The ruling class will think I am on their side
And make friendly overtures, but I shall retire
To the side further from Picra and write some poems
    About the doom of the whole boiling.

Anyone happy in this age and place
Is daft or corrupt. Better to abdicate
From a material and spiritual terrain
    Fit only for barbarians.

The Ides of March

Fireballs and thunder augment the wailing wind:
A vulgar score, but not inappropriate
To my romantic, classic situation.
Within the house my wife is asleep and dreaming
That I, too, am cocooned inside the world
Of love whose fear is that the other world
Will end it. But I wait uneasy here
Under the creaking trees, the low dark sky,
For the conspirators. This is the place
Where I come, in better weather, with a book
Or pen and paper – for I must confess
To a little amateur scribbling. Love and letters:
One ought to be content – would, if the times
Were different; if state and man were free,
The slaves fed well, and wars hung over us
Not with death's certainty but with the odds
Merely of dying a not too painful death.
Yes, I have caught the times like a disease
Whose remedy is still experimental;
And felt the times as some enormous gaffe
I cannot forget. And now I am about
To cease being a fellow traveller, about
To select from several complex panaceas,
Like a shy man confronted with a box
Of chocolates, the plainest after all.
I am aware that in my conscious wish
To rid the empire of a tyrant there
Is something that will give me personal pleasure;
That usually one's father's death occurs
About the time one becomes oneself a father.
These subtleties are not, I think, important –
No more than that I shall become a traitor,
Technically, to my class, my friend, my country.
No, the important thing is to remove
Guilt from this orchard, which is why I have
Invited here those men of action with

Their simpler motives and their naked knives.
I hope my wife will walk out of the house
While I am in their compromising presence,
And know that what we built had no foundation
Other than luck and my false privileged rôle
In a society that I despised.
And then society itself, aghast,
Reeling against the statue, also will
Be shocked to think I had a secret passion.
Though passion is, of course, not quite the word:
I merely choose what history foretells.
The dawn comes moonlike now between the trees
And silhouettes some rather muffled figures.
It is embarrassing to find oneself
Involved in this clumsy masquerade. There still
Is time to send a servant with a message:
'Brutus is not at home': time to postpone
Relief and fear. Yet, plucking nervously
The pregnant twigs, I stay. Good morning, comrades.

Autobiography of a Lungworm

My normal dwelling is the lungs of swine,
    My normal shape a worm,
But other dwellings, other shapes, are mine
    Within my natural term.
Dimly I see my life, of all, the sign,
    Of better lives the germ.

The pig, though I am inoffensive, coughs,
    Finding me irritant:
My eggs go with the contents of the troughs
    From mouth to excrement –
The pig thus thinks, perhaps, he forever doffs
    His niggling resident.

The eggs lie unconsidered in the dung
    Upon the farmyard floor,
Far from the scarlet and sustaining lung:
    But happily a poor
And humble denizen provides a rung
    To make ascension sure.

The earthworm eats the eggs; inside the warm
    Cylinder larvae hatch:
For years, if necessary, in this form
    I wait the lucky match
That will return me to my cherished norm,
    My ugly pelt dispatch.

Strangely, it is the pig himself becomes
    The god inside the car:
His greed devours the earthworms; so the slums
    Of his intestines are
The setting for the act when clay succumbs
    And force steers for its star.

The larvae burrow through the bowel wall
    And, having to the dregs
Drained ignominy, gain the lung's great hall.
    They change. Once more, like pegs,
Lungworms are anchored to the rise and fall
    – And start to lay their eggs.

What does this mean? The individual,
    Nature, mutation, strife?
I feel, though I am simple, still the whole
    Is complex; and that life –
A huge, doomed throbbing – has a wiry soul
    That must escape the knife.

Homage to Balthus

What a relief to admit, as Balthus
  with his paintings, that one's poems
are utter failures, without exception.
  Even to have got down, somewhere
along your life, the continuous line
  a girl's hair makes with her arm or
the revealed white band between naked thighs
  – quite pointless in the context of
possibilities. And the small figure
  walking away on the far green
cliff while we ourselves, trivial giants
  in the foreground, watch the artist;
and to light the outflung nude the curtain
  snatched back by a big-headed dwarf;
and in a tinted street the blanched plasterer . . .
  Noble artist, it cannot be
the absence of strange intimations
  in wide reality that you
lament but the eternal refusal
  of pigment, canvas, brush to make
a world parallel to blind creation
  and replace that with its order.

Notes

TRANSLATION. The title is a joke: the poem is not a translation of an existing poem in a foreign language, but is written as if it were, using a classical Latin form (so-called 'sapphics', consisting of three long lines followed by a shorter one), which was much used by the Roman poet Horace among others. The flavour of this imagined poet, however, is much more that of someone during the later Roman Empire, four or five hundred years after Horace, who is lamenting the decline of culture and civilisation. References which could have been used by such a poet — to slaves and barbarians, for example — are mixed with contemporary ones, such as 'the twelve-tone scale' (pioneered by certain twentieth-century musicians) and 'quarterlies/Devoted to daring verse'. The impression is of a pessimistic poet who chooses to stand aloof from the times he lives in, in the ironical belief that things have passed him by. Fuller adopts the mask of such a man to comment on the dilemmas of our own day. One could compare this poem with some written by the modern Greek poet, Cavafy (died 1930), who wrote in similar terms about the dying Graeco-Roman world and the coming of the barbarians. Cinna (the name Fuller chooses) is the name of the poet in Shakespeare's *Julius Caesar* who is torn apart by the mob, partly because of his 'bad verses'.

THE IDES OF MARCH. It was a risky enterprise for Fuller to have attempted a monologue for Brutus, especially in blank verse; one is bound to be reminded of what Shakespeare did. But Fuller succeeds, partly because (in spite of the convincing 'period' setting) he gives his Brutus a modern sensibility: the irresolution of the speaker is of a different kind from that of an antique Roman, or of Shakespeare's Brutus.

AUTOBIOGRAPHY OF A LUNGWORM. Many of Fuller's poems draw on his wide and catholic reading, of history (including ancient history), musicology, anthropology, science, and in particular natural history and biology. The actual details of the life process of the lungworm are accurate. One of the twists that

Fuller gives to the straight facts is to make the poem into a monologue, but one that could not be more different from Brutus's in 'The Ides of March'. And part of the cyclical inevitability of what is said by the creature comes from the formal repetition, each stanza rhyming on the pattern *ab ab ab*.

HOMAGE TO BALTHUS. This seems a case of the artist confronting and acknowledging his failure. The French painter Balthus (1908–   ) is not alone among artists in finally condemning his own work: the Italian Chirico did the same. The falling-short suggested in the poem is between achievement and 'possibilities'; the impossibility of translating the 'strange intimations/in wide reality' into the actual representation with the artist's materials, whether 'pigment, canvas, brush' or words. In what way is it 'a relief to admit' this?

R. S. Thomas

R. S. Thomas was born in 1913 and ordained a priest in 1937. In 1977, he retired after forty years' service in his native Wales. Much of his poetry has been, in the true sense of the word, *parochial* – concerned with the inhabitants and bleak landscapes of the Welsh hill country – and until the publication of his collection *H'm* (1972) it was anchored in the bedrock of naturalistic description. More recently he has enlarged his range so that each new poem seems to become a continuation of what he calls the 'linguistic confrontation with ultimate reality', a kind of contentious struggling through paradox after paradox with a saviour who has all the odds. This development has been accompanied by a greater reliance on the effect of cadence and modulation in the making of a poem, and rather less on the impact of metaphor. Whether or not this indicates a failure of the poetic imagination is a question lying at the centre of much of the debate about Thomas's recent work, from which we have taken the six poems printed here.

Gone?

Will they say on some future
occasion, looking over the flogged acres
of ploughland: This was Prytherch country?
Nothing to show for it now: hedges
uprooted, walls gone, a mobile people
hurrying to and fro on their fast
tractors; a forest of aerials
as though an invading fleet invisibly
had come to anchor among these
financed hills. They copy the image
of themselves projected on their smooth
screens to the accompaniment of inane
music. They give grins and smiles
back in return for the money that is
spent on them. But where is the face
with the crazed eyes that through the unseen
drizzle of its tears looked out
on this land and found no beauty
in it, but accepted it, as a man
will who has needs in him that only
bare ground, black thorns and the sky's
                    emptiness can fulfil?

Album

My father is dead.
I who am look at him
who is not, as once he
went looking for me
in the woman who was.

There are pictures
of the two of them, no
need of a third, hand
in hand, hearts willing
to be one but not three.

What does it mean
life? I am here I am
there. Look! Suddenly
the young tool in their hands
for hurting one another.

And the camera says:
Smile; there is no wound
time gives that is not bandaged
by time. And so they do the
three of them at me who weep.

The Moon in Lleyn

The last quarter of the moon
of Jesus gives way
to the dark; the serpent
digests the egg. Here
on my knees in this stone
church, that is full only
of the silent congregation
of shadows and the sea's
sound, it is easy to believe
Yeats was right. Just as though
choirs had not sung, shells
have swallowed them; the tide laps
at the Bible; the bell fetches
no people to the brittle miracle
of the bread. The sand is waiting
for the running back of the grains
in the wall into its blond
glass. Religion is over, and
what will emerge from the body
of the new moon, no one
can say.

      But a voice sounds
in my ear: Why so fast,
mortal? These very seas
are baptized. The parish
has a saint's name time cannot
unfrock. In cities that
have outgrown their promise people
are becoming pilgrims
again, if not to this place,
then to the recreation of it
in their own spirits. You must remain
kneeling. Even as this moon
making its way through the earth's
cumbersome shadow, prayer, too,
has its phases.

The Chapel

A little aside from the main road,
becalmed in a last-century greyness,
there is the chapel, ugly, without the appeal
to the tourist to stop his car
and visit it. The traffic goes by,
and the river goes by, and quick shadows
of clouds, too, and the chapel settles
a little deeper into the grass.

But here once on an evening like this,
in the darkness that was about
his hearers, a preacher caught fire
and burned steadily before them
with a strange light, so that they saw
the splendour of the barren mountains
about them and sang their amens
fiercely, narrow but saved
in a way that men are not now.

The Bright Field

I have seen the sun break through
to illuminate a small field
for a while, and gone my way
and forgotten it. But that was the pearl
of great price, the one field that had
the treasure in it. I realize now
that I must give all that I have
to possess it. Life is not hurrying

on to a receding future, nor hankering after
an imagined past. It is the turning
aside like Moses to the miracle
of the lit bush, to a brightness
that seemed as transitory as your youth
once, but is the eternity that awaits you.

Groping

Moving away is only to the boundaries
of the self. Better to stay here,
I said, leaving the horizons
clear. The best journey to make
is inward. It is the interior
that calls. Eliot heard it.
Wordsworth turned from the great hills
of the north to the precipice
of his own mind, and let himself
down for the poetry stranded
on the bare ledges.
                                        For some
it is all darkness; for me, too,
it is dark. But there are hands
there I can take, voices to hear
solider than the echoes
without. And sometimes a strange light
shines, purer than the moon,
casting no shadow, that is
the halo upon the bones
of the pioneers who died for truth.

Notes

GONE? This bleak vision of a possible future, though consistent in its style with all Thomas's more recent poems, makes a link with his earlier work in that it is concerned with the Welsh hill country — 'Prytherch country', in fact: in many earlier poems Thomas used this Welsh surname as a name for the typical inhabitant, the 'poor farmer with no name' who is addressed in 'The Dark Well', 'Too Late', 'Portrait', 'Servant' and other poems in *Tares* (1961) and *The Bread of Truth* (1963).

ALBUM. This stark and moving poem has all the exquisitely painful mystery of a life coming clear in the developing-tray. It is spare but remorselessly observant. Notice how the third stanza introduces a note of drama and amazement: the exclamation, and the poem's only immediate conjunction of adjective and noun. In a poem as closely written as this it is often rewarding to consider the 'meaning' revealed by syntax.

THE MOON IN LLEYN. The setting of this poem is the Lleyn Peninsula in Wales where, during the later years of his ministry, Thomas was vicar of the small parish of Aberdaron. Several late-nineteenth and twentieth century poets have written rather ponderously about the imminent collapse of Western Civilization, but here Thomas balances parochial observation and the global speculation it gives rise to. A phrase such as 'the brittle miracle of the bread' suggests at once the crisp thinness of the communion wafer and the preciousness of the sacrament it embodies, the faith it symbolises. The reference to Yeats concerns that poet's cyclical view of history, deriving from his concept of a Great Wheel and the Phases of the Moon. This makes fascinating, though often obscure, reading in its own right, but here it is enough to recognise that — according to Yeats's theory — we are now reaching the end of one historical revolution of the Wheel. Each revolution should take, Yeats says, about two thousand years and will end in a chaos which begets a new pattern of civilization. Thus, as we approach the year 2000, we are coming close to the end of the Christian 'cycle'. A sympathetic response to — even a provisional sharing of — this view lies behind the first section of Thomas's poem. The second section needs no gloss, but it might be interesting to compare the statements it makes with those to be found in the closing stanzas of Philip Larkin's 'Church Going'.

THE CHAPEL. Those who find too much dryness – both of movement and of spirit – in Thomas's work should consider this poem. The humdrum detail and dismissiveness of the first eight lines are at once underlined and alleviated by the rapid lyrical movement of:

>The traffic goes by,
and the river goes by, and quick shadows
of clouds, too, and the chapel settles
a little deeper into the grass.

Then, in cadences that are both anecdotal and exalted, the power and passion of the evangelical preacher from the past are celebrated – to be checked, with plain resignation, by the eight monosyllables of the final line.

THE BRIGHT FIELD. Beginning with the book called *H'm*, published in 1972, Thomas has refined his poems to statements that are both very plain and challengingly intense. They are confrontations with God or no-God, faith or lack of faith; meditations on and arguments about human and spiritual existence; sometimes brief parables or fables. Though arranged in a set of eight lines and then six, as a sonnet, 'The Bright Field' has no regular metrical or rhymed structure, and the breaks between the lines seem to have no significance. Yet read it aloud and it is certainly not prose, nor are the plain assertions just plain.

GROPING. Some of Thomas's critics have regretted his recent, often somewhat abstract, or universalised, response to 'the interior/ that calls'. They prefer his ploughing of a straight, recognisable hill-country furrow to the kind of groping he speaks of in this poem. Like Wordsworth, though, he has become increasingly preoccupied with scaling the 'precipice of his own mind' and at the centre of his later work there is what he has called 'a confrontation with ultimate reality' which recalls several of the metaphysical poets of the seventeenth century, particularly George Herbert.

Charles Causley

Charles Causley was born in Cornwall in 1917 and, apart from the time spent serving in the Royal Navy during the war, has lived there all his life. Until his retirement, he worked as a school teacher in his home town of Launceston. His poetry emerges, interestingly, from the close pattern of his life. The sea is often present in it, as also are the landmarks and customs of Cornwall, and much of it is marked by a brisk directness as well as skilful variations on familiar ballad-style rhythms. These ingredients have made it deservedly popular, not least with younger readers, for whom Causley has written several books of verse, including the delightful *Figgie Hobbin* (available as a Puffin paperback). It would be a mistake to see him only as a balladmonger, however. His *Collected Poems 1951–1975* (Macmillan) is an impressively varied volume and contains accomplished writing in free verse as well as rhymed poetry of a mysterious depth and resonance.

My Friend Maloney

My friend Maloney, eighteen,
   Swears like a sentry,
Got into trouble two years back
   With the local gentry.

Parson and squire's sons
   Informed a copper.
The magistrate took one look at Maloney.
   Fixed him proper.

Talked of the crime of youth,
   The innocent victim.
Maloney never said a blind word
   To contradict him.

Maloney of Gun Street,
   Back of the Nuclear Mission,
Son of the town whore,
   Blamed television.

Justice, as usual, triumphed.
   Everyone felt fine.
Things went deader.
   Maloney went up the line.

Maloney learned one lesson:
   Never play the fool
With the products of especially a minor
   Public school.

Maloney lost a thing or two
   At that institution.
First shirt, second innocence,
   The old irresolution.

Found himself a girl-friend,
   Sharp suit, sharp collars.
Maloney on a moped,
   Pants full of dollars.

College boys on the corner
   In striped, strait blazers
Look at old Maloney,
   Eyes like razors.

You don't need talent, says Maloney.
   You don't need looks.
All I got you got, fellers.
   You can keep your thick books.

Parson got religion,
   Squire, in the end, the same.
The magistrate went over the wall.
   Life, said Maloney,'s a game.

Consider then the case of Maloney,
   College boys, parson, squire, beak.
Who was the victor and who was the victim?
   Speak.

By St Thomas Water

By St Thomas Water
Where the river is thin
We looked for a jam-jar
To catch the quick fish in.
Through St Thomas Church-yard
Jessie and I ran
The day we took the jam-pot
Off the dead man.

On the scuffed tombstone
The grey flowers fell,
Cracked was the water,
Silent the shell.
The snake for an emblem
Swirled on the slab,
Across the beach of sky the sun
Crawled like a crab.

'If we walk,' said Jessie,
'Seven times round.
We shall hear a dead man
Speaking underground.'
Round the stone we danced, we sang.
Watched the sun drop,
Laid our heads and listened
At the tomb-top.

Soft as the thunder
At the storm's start
I heard a voice as clear as blood.
Strong as the heart.
But what words were spoken
I can never say,
I shut my fingers round my head,
Drove them away.

'What are those letters, Jessie,
Cut so sharp and trim
All round this holy stone
With earth up to the brim?'
Jessie traced the letters
Black as coffin-lead.
'He is not dead but sleeping.'
Slowly she said.

I looked at Jessie,
Jessie looked at me,
And our eyes in wonder
Grew wide as the sea.
Past the green and bending stones
We fled hand in hand,
Silent through the tongues of grass
To the river strand.

By the creaking cypress
We moved as soft as smoke
For fear all the people
Underneath awoke.
Over all the sleepers
We darted light as snow
In case they opened up their eyes,
Called us from below.

Many a day has faltered
Into many a year
Since the dead awoke and spoke
And we would not hear.
Waiting in the cold grass
Under a crinkled bough,
Quiet stone, cautious stone,
What do you tell me now?

Reservoir Street

In nineteen twenty-six, the year
Of the Strike, on a day of bubbling heat
I went to stay with my sun-faced cousins
Who lived in a house on Reservoir Street.

Auntie stood strong as the Eddystone Lighthouse.
A terrible light shone out of her head.
Her children scuttled like ships for harbour.
You must let them know what's what, she said.

Her five prime-beef boys circled round me.
They didn't enjoy what they saw at all.
We couldn't make any more of each other
Than the map of stains on the bedroom wall.

All night long on the road to the city
The motor-car tyres rubbed out the dark.
Early in the morning I watched from the window
The sun like a killer come out of the park.

Down in the reservoir I saw a man drowning.
His flooding head came over the side.
They poked him out of a parcel of water.
He's poisoned the drink! my cousins cried.

I packed my bag and I said to Auntie,
I think I'll go home on the one o'clock train.
My, they all said, he wants his mammy.
They never let me forget it again.

Through the Cornish jungle-country
Like a parrot the train screamed home.
I thought of my brother who slept beside me,
Four walls round us pure as cloam.

When I got to the house my head was thunder.
The bed lay open as a shell.
Sweet was my brother's kiss, and sweeter
The innocent water from the well.

Conducting a Children's Choir

They hold before their faces masks of flowers.
Their summer eyes anticipate the snow.
In skin as yet untouched by ticking showers
There lies the simple statement of the crow.

Meanwhile an audience, quite unaware
Of certain cunning, ancient as the Cave,
Observes the seraphim on sands of prayer,
Oblivious of each black, unbalanced wave.

The voices scale the trim, Italian airs,
Assail the senses with a brilliant pain.
Under my palm a calm corruption wears
An innocence articulate as rain.

I bait the snapping breath, curled claw, the deep
And delicate tongue that lends no man its aid.
The children their unsmiling kingdoms keep,
And I walk with them, and I am afraid.

Notes

MY FRIEND MALONEY. *Whose* friend? A terse, in places almost telegrammatic, ballad about a completely unsentimental education. The reader is exhorted to examine a life history and ask some serious questions. Indeed, to *answer* them: it is hard to wriggle off the monosyllabic hook of that final 'Speak'. Much will be gained by reading this poem aloud and striking the balance between pulpit and barrack-room. Causley has shown a considerable talent for working a variety of contemporary voices into the traditional ballad form, and this mixing of new material with familiar patterns largely accounts for his deserved popularity. In the penultimate verse, 'over the wall' means 'to gaol: sentenced to detention barracks'.

BY ST THOMAS WATER. A childhood incident enlarges, through recollection, to a meditation on death. The children's thrilled sense of awe and their self-induced fear of the dead is subtly built up, and it can be noticed how the images of stone and grass recur. These chart the shift from careless youth to contemplative age – the tongues of grass become 'cold', telling a different tale ('under a *crinkled* bough'), and the stone around which the children danced and sang becomes 'quiet' and 'cautious' as its message 'He is not dead but sleeping' takes on a real and darker meaning for the older poet. The scene of the poem is only a hundred yards from Riverside, Launceston, Causley's birthplace, and the 'speaking' stone still stands in St Thomas church-yard.

RESERVOIR STREET. This poem is striking for the grim humour with which Causley recalls a brief stay with his Aunt and cousins. Despite the emphasis on the sun in the first four stanzas, it is an unsympathetic, hard (killer) light which casts a long shadow. Auntie's implacable, pragmatic virtue is brilliantly captured by the image of the Eddystone Lighthouse – the light of which is a warning and can be seen up to seventeen and a half miles away! The fifth stanza has the unexplained discontinuity of nightmare and becomes the turning point of the poem: his

69

cousins' reaction defines all that Causley found unsympathetic about them — the gulf between his nervous imagination and their 'prime-beef' insensitivity. The final stanza beautifully depicts the sweet reclamation of a secure home. 'The Strike' (stanza 1) refers to the General Strike of 1926, and 'cloam' (stanza 7) is the clay used for making an earthenware oven built into the side of an old-fashioned open hearth.

CONDUCTING A CHILDREN'S CHOIR. Charles Causley has taught children for much of his life, and no good teacher is ever sentimental about children. This poem leaves all unthinking adulation to the concert audience which looks on the choristers as seraphim (celestial beings associated with light and purity). The poet himself, while keeping time as a conductor, meditates upon time and the mortal conspiracy which links him to the children. The 'simple statement of the crow' refers to crowsfeet, the lines of age which appear round the eyes, and notice how even the showers 'tick'. The poem is full of finely judged associations, as for example in the use of the word 'wave' to suggest at once the sea, the unconscious mind and the wave of sound which comes from the singers.

Philip Larkin

Philip Larkin was born in 1922. He works as a librarian, for the past twenty-five years as Librarian of the University of Hull. Although he published a book of poems and two novels in the 1940s, he first attracted wide attention with *The Less Deceived* in 1955. This book quickly established Larkin as an outstanding poet of the post-war period, writing work which imprinted itself effortlessly on the memory. Each of his mature books has included one long poem which seems to sum up an area of concern: 'Church Going' in *The Less Deceived*, 'The Whitsun Weddings' in the book of that title (1964), and 'The Building' in *High Windows* (1974). But apart from these major statements, all included in this selection, there are many shorter poems which look at kindred themes of time passing, disappointment, loneliness, balanced with their opposites – permanence, joy (however brief), the sharing of some ritual (as in 'To the Sea' and 'Show Saturday', both in *High Windows*). One of Larkin's special gifts has been seen to be the celebrating, the making beautiful, of subject-matter that would conventionally be seen as hopeless, depressing, and negative. Although Larkin's poems do not show any obvious or startling technical trickeries, they have an astonishing adroitness and exactness if one looks at them closely, a weaving together of sound and sense which is, in the best meaning of the word, 'refined'.

Love Songs in Age

She kept her songs, they took so little space,
    The covers pleased her:
One bleached from lying in a sunny place,
One marked in circles by a vase of water,
One mended, when a tidy fit had seized her,
    And coloured, by her daughter –
So they had waited, till in widowhood
She found them, looking for something else, and stood

Relearning how each frank submissive chord
    Had ushered in
Word after sprawling hyphenated word,
And the unfailing sense of being young
Spread out like a spring-woken tree, wherein
    That hidden freshness sung,
That certainty of time laid up in store
As when she played them first. But, even more,

The glare of that much-mentioned brilliance, love,
    Broke out, to show
Its bright incipience sailing above,
Still promising to solve, and satisfy,
And set unchangeably in order. So
    To pile them back, to cry,
Was hard, without lamely admitting how
It had not done so then, and could not now.

Ambulances

Closed like confessionals, they thread
Loud noons of cities, giving back
None of the glances they absorb.
Light glossy grey, arms on a plaque,
They come to rest at any kerb:
All streets in time are visited.

Then children strewn on steps or road,
Or women coming from the shops
Past smells of different dinners, see
A wild white face that overtops
Red stretcher-blankets momently
As it is carried in and stowed,

And sense the solving emptiness
That lies just under all we do,
And for a second get it whole,
So permanent and blank and true.
The fastened doors recede. *Poor soul*,
They whisper at their own distress;

For borne away in deadened air
May go the sudden shut of loss
Round something nearly at an end,
And what cohered in it across
The years, the unique random blend
Of families and fashions, there

At last begin to loosen. Far
From the exchange of love to lie
Unreachable inside a room
The traffic parts to let go by
Brings closer what is left to come,
And dulls to distance all we are.

The Old Fools

What do they think has happened, the old fools,
To make them like this? Do they somehow suppose
It's more grown-up when your mouth hangs open and drools,
And you keep on pissing yourself, and can't remember
Who called this morning? Or that, if they only chose,
They could alter things back to when they danced all night,
Or went to their wedding, or sloped arms some September?
Or do they fancy there's really been no change,
And they've always behaved as if they were crippled or tight,
Or sat through days of thin continuous dreaming
Watching light move? If they don't (and they can't), it's
                                                    strange:

    Why aren't they screaming?

At death, you break up: the bits that were you
Start speeding away from each other for ever
With no one to see. It's only oblivion, true:
We had it before, but then it was going to end,
And was all the time merging with a unique endeavour
To bring to bloom the million-petalled flower
Of being here. Next time you can't pretend
There'll be anything else. And these are the first signs:
Not knowing how, not hearing who, the power
Of choosing gone. Their looks show that they're for it:
Ash hair, toad hands, prune face dried into lines –
    How can they ignore it?

Perhaps being old is having lighted rooms
Inside your head, and people in them, acting.
People you know, yet can't quite name; each looms
Like a deep loss restored, from known doors turning,
Setting down a lamp, smiling from a stair, extracting
A known book from the shelves; or sometimes only

The rooms themselves, chairs and a fire burning,
The blown bush at the window, or the sun's
Faint friendliness on the wall some lonely
Rain-ceased midsummer evening. That is where they live:
Not here and now, but where all happened once.
      This is why they give

An air of baffled absence, trying to be there
Yet being here. For the rooms grow farther, leaving
Incompetent cold, the constant wear and tear
Of taken breath, and them crouching below
Extinction's alp, the old fools, never perceiving
How near it is. This must be what keeps them quiet:
The peak that stays in view wherever we go
For them is rising ground. Can they never tell
What is dragging them back, and how it will end? Not at
                                   night?
Not when the strangers come? Never, throughout
The whole hideous inverted childhood? Well,
      We shall find out.

The Building

Higher than the handsomest hotel
The lucent comb shows up for miles, but see,
All round it close-ribbed streets rise and fall
Like a great sigh out of the last century.
The porters are scruffy; what keep drawing up
At the entrance are not taxis; and in the hall
As well as creepers hangs a frightening smell.

There are paperbacks, and tea at so much a cup,
Like an airport lounge, but those who tamely sit
On rows of steel chairs turning the ripped mags
Haven't come far. More like a local bus,
These outdoor clothes and half-filled shopping bags
And faces restless and resigned, although
Every few minutes comes a kind of nurse

To fetch someone away: the rest refit
Cups back to saucers, cough, or glance below
Seats for dropped gloves or cards. Humans, caught
On ground curiously neutral, homes and names
Suddenly in abeyance; some are young,
Some old, but most at that vague age that claims
The end of choice, the last of hope; and all

Here to confess that something has gone wrong.
It must be error of a serious sort,
For see how many floors it needs, how tall
It's grown by now, and how much money goes
In trying to correct it. See the time,
Half-past eleven on a working day,
And these picked out of it; see, as they climb

To their appointed levels, how their eyes
Go to each other, guessing; on the way
Someone's wheeled past, in washed-to-rags ward clothes:
They see him, too. They're quiet. To realise
This new thing held in common makes them quiet,
For past these doors are rooms, and rooms past those,
And more rooms yet, each one further off

And harder to return from; and who knows
Which he will see, and when ? For the moment, wait,
Look down at the yard. Outside seems old enough:
Red brick, lagged pipes, and someone walking by it
Out to the car park, free. Then, past the gate,
Traffic; a locked church; short terraced streets
Where kids chalk games, and girls with hair-dos fetch

Their separates from the cleaners – O world,
Your loves, your chances, are beyond the stretch
Of any hand from here! And so, unreal,
A touching dream to which we all are lulled
But wake from separately. In it, conceits
And self-protecting ignorance congeal
To carry life, collapsing only when

Called to these corridors (for now once more
The nurse beckons –). Each gets up and goes
At last. Some will be out by lunch, or four;
Others, not knowing it, have come to join
The unseen congregations whose white rows
Lie set apart above – women, men;
Old, young; crude facets of the only coin

This place accepts. All know they are going to die.
Not yet, perhaps not here, but in the end,
And somewhere like this. That is what it means,
This clean-sliced cliff; a struggle to transcend
The thought of dying, for unless its powers
Outbuild cathedrals nothing contravenes
The coming dark, though crowds each evening try

With wasteful, weak, propitiatory flowers.

The Whitsun Weddings

That Whitsun, I was late getting away:
  Not till about
One-twenty on the sunlit Saturday
Did my three-quarters-empty train pull out,
All windows down, all cushions hot, all sense
Of being in a hurry gone. We ran
Behind the backs of houses, crossed a street
Of blinding windscreens, smelt the fish-dock; thence
The river's level drifting breadth began,
Where sky and Lincolnshire and water meet.

All afternoon, through the tall heat that slept
  For miles inland,
A slow and stopping curve southwards we kept.
Wide farms went by, short-shadowed cattle, and
Canals with floatings of industrial froth;
A hothouse flashed uniquely: hedges dipped
And rose: and now and then a smell of grass
Displaced the reek of buttoned carriage-cloth
Until the next town, new and nondescript,
Approached with acres of dismantled cars.

At first, I didn't notice what a noise
  The weddings made
Each station that we stopped at: sun destroys
The interest of what's happening in the shade,
And down the long cool platforms whoops and skirls
I took for porters larking with the mails,
And went on reading. Once we started, though,
We passed them, grinning and pomaded, girls
In parodies of fashion, heels and veils,
All posed irresolutely, watching us go,

As if out on the end of an event
   Waving goodbye
To something that survived it. Struck, I leant
More promptly out next time, more curiously,
And saw it all again in different terms:
The fathers with broad belts under their suits
And seamy foreheads; mothers loud and fat;
An uncle shouting smut; and then the perms,
The nylon gloves and jewellery-substitutes,
The lemons, mauves, and olive-ochres that

Marked off the girls unreally from the rest.
   Yes, from cafés
And banquet-halls up yards, and bunting-dressed
Coach-party annexes, the wedding-days
Were coming to an end. All down the line
Fresh couples climbed aboard: the rest stood round;
The last confetti and advice were thrown,
And, as we moved, each face seemed to define
Just what it saw departing: children frowned
At something dull; fathers had never known

Success so huge and wholly farcical;
   The women shared
The secret like a happy funeral;
While girls, gripping their handbags tighter, stared
At a religious wounding. Free at last,
And loaded with the sum of all they saw,
We hurried towards London, shuffling gouts of steam.
Now fields were building-plots, and poplars cast
Long shadows over major roads, and for
Some fifty minutes, that in time would seem

Just long enough to settle hats and say
  I nearly died,
A dozen marriages got under way.
They watched the landscape, sitting side by side
– An Odeon went past, a cooling tower,
And someone running up to bowl – and none
Thought of the others they would never meet
Or how their lives would all contain this hour.
I thought of London spread out in the sun,
Its postal districts packed like squares of wheat:

There we were aimed. And as we raced across
  Bright knots of rail
Past standing Pullmans, walls of blackened moss
Came close, and it was nearly done, this frail
Travelling coincidence; and what it held
Stood ready to be loosed with all the power
That being changed can give. We slowed again,
And as the tightened brakes took hold, there swelled
A sense of falling, like an arrow-shower
Sent out of sight, somewhere becoming rain.

An Arundel Tomb

Side by side, their faces blurred,
The earl and countess lie in stone,
Their proper habits vaguely shown
As jointed armour, stiffened pleat,
And that faint hint of the absurd –
The little dogs under their feet.

Such plainness of the pre-baroque
Hardly involves the eye, until
It meets his left-hand gauntlet, still
Clasped empty in the other; and
One sees, with a sharp tender shock,
His hand withdrawn, holding her hand.

They would not think to lie so long.
Such faithfulness in effigy
Was just a detail friends would see:
A sculptor's sweet commissioned grace
Thrown off in helping to prolong
The Latin names around the base.

They would not guess how early in
Their supine stationary voyage
The air would change to soundless damage,
Turn the old tenantry away;
How soon succeeding eyes begin
To look, not read. Rigidly they

Persisted, linked, through lengths and breadths
Of time. Snow fell, undated. Light
Each summer thronged the glass. A bright
Litter of birdcalls strewed the same
Bone-riddled ground. And up the paths
The endless altered people came,

Washing at their identity.
Now, helpless in the hollow of
An unarmorial age, a trough
Of smoke in slow suspended skeins
Above their scrap of history,
Only an attitude remains:

Time has transfigured them into
Untruth. The stone fidelity
They hardly meant has come to be
Their final blazon, and to prove
Our almost-instinct almost true:
What will survive of us is love.

The Explosion

On the day of the explosion
Shadows pointed towards the pithead:
In the sun the slagheap slept.

Down the lane came men in pitboots
Coughing oath-edged talk and pipe-smoke,
Shouldering off the freshened silence.

One chased after rabbits; lost them;
Came back with a nest of lark's eggs;
Showed them; lodged them in the grasses.

So they passed in beards and moleskins,
Fathers, brothers, nicknames, laughter,
Through the tall gates standing open.

At noon, there came a tremor; cows
Stopped chewing for a second; sun,
Scarfed as in a heat-haze, dimmed.

The dead go on before us, they
Are sitting in God's house in comfort,
We shall see them face to face —

Plain as lettering in the chapels
It was said, and for a second
Wives saw men of the explosion

Larger than in life they managed —
Gold as on a coin, or walking
Somehow from the sun towards them,

One showing the eggs unbroken.

Church Going

Once I am sure there's nothing going on
I step inside, letting the door thud shut.
Another church: matting, seats, and stone,
And little books; sprawlings of flowers, cut
For Sunday, brownish now; some brass and stuff
Up at the holy end; the small neat organ;
And a tense, musty, unignorable silence,
Brewed God knows how long. Hatless, I take off
My cycle-clips in awkward reverence,

Move forward, run my hand around the font.
From where I stand, the roof looks almost new –
Cleaned, or restored? Someone would know: I don't.
Mounting the lectern, I peruse a few
Hectoring large-scale verses, and pronounce
'Here endeth' much more loudly than I'd meant.
The echoes snigger briefly. Back at the door
I sign the book, donate an Irish sixpence,
Reflect the place was not worth stopping for.

Yet stop I did: in fact I often do,
And always end much at a loss like this,
Wondering what to look for; wondering, too,
When churches fall completely out of use
What we shall turn them into, if we shall keep
A few cathedrals chronically on show,
Their parchment, plate and pyx in locked cases,
And let the rest rent-free to rain and sheep.
Shall we avoid them as unlucky places?

Or, after dark, will dubious women come
To make their children touch a particular stone;
Pick simples for a cancer; or on some
Advised night see walking a dead one?
Power of some sort or other will go on
In games, in riddles, seemingly at random;
But superstition, like belief, must die,
And what remains when disbelief has gone?
Grass, weedy pavement, brambles, buttress, sky,

A shape less recognisable each week,
A purpose more obscure. I wonder who
Will be the last, the very last, to seek
This place for what it was; one of the crew
That tap and jot and know what rood-lofts were?
Some ruin-bibber, randy for antique,
Or Christmas-addict, counting on a whiff
Of gowns-and-bands and organ-pipes and myrrh?
Or will he be my representative,

Bored, uninformed, knowing the ghostly silt
Dispersed, yet tending to this cross of ground
Through suburb scrub because it held unspilt
So long and equably what since is found
Only in separation – marriage, and birth,
And death, and thoughts of these – for which was built
This special shell? For, though I've no idea
What this accoutred frowsty barn is worth,
It pleases me to stand in silence here;

A serious house on serious earth it is,
In whose blent air all our compulsions meet,
Are recognised, and robed as destinies.
And that much never can be obsolete,
Since someone will forever be surprising
A hunger in himself to be more serious,
And gravitating with it to this ground,
Which, he once heard, was proper to grow wise in,
If only that so many dead lie round.

The Trees

The trees are coming into leaf
Like something almost being said;
The recent buds relax and spread,
Their greenness is a kind of grief.

Is it that they are born again
And we grow old? No, they die too.
Their yearly trick of looking new
Is written down in rings of grain.

Yet still the unresting castles thresh
In fullgrown thickness every May.
Last year is dead, they seem to say,
Begin afresh, afresh, afresh.

Notes

LOVE SONGS IN AGE. A woman in widowhood finds the sheet music of love songs she used to play and sing when she was a girl, and sharply realises that 'love' is an empty promise, offering more than it can ever give. Notice how the three sentences of the poem gradually narrow down: the detail and the lyricism are expansive, the words and rhythms acting imitatively ('Word after sprawling hyphenated word' describes the way the song is laid out on the sheet music); then 'The glare of that much-mentioned brilliance, love' illuminates the plain and seeming inevitability of what it promised; finally, there is the blank acknowledgement of the final line, a series of monosyllables which hammer home the disappointment.

AMBULANCES. The unusual notion on which this poem is based is that ambulances are seen as messengers of death, not of mercy: they are reminders of 'what is left to come', 'the solving emptiness/That lies just under all we do'. There is something sinister about them, in their self-contained separateness, and they are described as if they were self-willed agents. The victim or patient is 'stowed' like a piece of cargo, or a corpse, as if life had already vanished; the air itself is 'deadened' or numbed, as if the ambulance were a coffin.

THE OLD FOOLS. The tone of the opening questions is rasping and exasperated, reducing the physical habits of senility – as seen, for example, in a 'home' for old people – to comparisons with the disgusting and pathetic behaviour of infants or drunks; and, like infants or drunks, part of the trouble is that the senile do not appear to know what impression they make on the observer. The intricate processes of life are seen, in the second stanza, as moving from oblivion to oblivion; and the 'first signs' of the second oblivion are the loss of both physical and mental powers. Memory is fitful, the past comes and goes randomly. Each intricately patterned stanza is dense with packed details, which float in and out of the continuing puzzled questions, the self-debate,

86

gradually losing that over-compensating exasperation as the realisation dawns that this process is something we shall all individually have to undergo. The short final line of each stanza seems to tug back the debate and sharpen it, preparing it for the concluding remorseless and grim statement.

THE BUILDING. In the opinion of many people, this is Larkin's best poem, in which his habitual theme of the ebbing-away of life is most persistently, elaborately and movingly worked out. The details of what is in fact a hospital are throughout presented at one remove, as it were; the 'building' is not specifically called a hospital anywhere in the poem, as if naming it would be to court disaster, though, ironically, the daily arrival of disaster – death – is what the poem is 'about'. If 'Church Going' is concerned with the ritualising of death and 'The Whitsun Weddings' with the ritualising of life, the continuity of life in marriage, then 'The Building' could be said to be concerned with the ritualising attempt to stop the process of life becoming death – doomed to failure, as 'wasteful, weak, propitiatory' as the flowers brought to the patients, themselves immediately reminiscent of the flowers placed on the graves of the dead. Religious connotations are apparent throughout: all are 'Here to *confess* that something has gone wrong', which must be '*error* of a serious sort'; 'The unseen *congregations*'; the powers of this building must 'Outbuild *cathedrals*' if they are to outface death; and the flowers themselves are 'propitiatory' – that is, attempts to appease or gain favour with a god or some other supreme force.

The stanzaic structure of 'The Building' is a good example of how tightly organised the technical mode is of many Larkin poems. Each seven-line stanza is completely consistent in its rhyme scheme, but the first line of each stanza picks up the rhyme in the fifth line of the stanza preceding it, so that the whole poem can be seen to be made up of interlinked quatrains (rhyming ABCB: DCAD), the 'trailing' rhyme picking up the serpentine movement and running it on. Larkin once said, in a humorously disparaging way, that writing poetry was 'like knitting'; and that remark is given serious force by the unobtrusive formal mastery of 'The Building'.

THE WHITSUN WEDDINGS. The journey is a literal one, faithfully documented from Hull to London, on a Whit Saturday – a popular time for weddings, shifting in the church calendar between May and June. The poem accumulates detail as it goes along just as the train accumulates passengers, and the controlled expansiveness of the stanza form helps this, with its fluidity between stanzas and with the short four-syllable second line acting as a pivot on which each stanza turns, pushing the poem forward to the next smooth run. The force is partly cumulative and, as in 'Church Going' and 'The Building', it can accommodate several tones, from amused descriptiveness to the mysterious gravity of the conclusion. The poignancy, almost the randomness, of human pairing and bonding in marriage is part of the 'frail/Travelling coincidence' that is life as well as a railway journey.

AN ARUNDEL TOMB. The medieval monument which was in Larkin's mind is in Chichester Cathedral. The tentativeness of the conclusion ('almost-instinct almost true') is delicately balanced against the plain assertion of the final line. One odd point: if (as some architectural scholars maintain, though Larkin did not know this at the time) the detail of the clasped hands is the work of a Victorian sculptor who restored the monument, does this affect the poem or not?

THE EXPLOSION. This is an unusual venture for Larkin in several ways. It describes a wholly externalised scene from the past (which one could compare with two poems not included here, 'MCMXIV' and 'The Card-Players'); it proceeds like an incident from a novel or story; and, technically, it uses a metre which Larkin employs nowhere else, one which is associated chiefly with a once-famous poem by the nineteenth-century American, Longfellow: 'Hiawatha'. Larkin himself, when choosing the poem to read in a broadcast, said it 'isn't especially like me, or like what I fancy I'm supposed to be like'. Nevertheless, the observed details – of the men, their actions, the explosion itself – have that mixture of casualness and accuracy which is very much Larkin's.

CHURCH GOING. The seven nine-line stanzas of this, probably still Larkin's best-known poem, are a gradual plotting of the 'hunger . . . to be more serious' touched on towards the end. The whole tone of the opening is anecdotally *un*serious, even supercilious. The actual function of the church, a place where services are held, seems alien to the speaker: he is wary that something might be 'going on', such as a service or a choir practice, and makes sure that nothing is before he ventures in. He wants the place to himself: once that is assured, he treats it with casual curiosity, listing its objects perfunctorily and dismissively – 'little books' (hymnbooks and prayerbooks), 'some brass and stuff/ Up at the holy end' (the crucifix and candles). But a vague respect, an 'awkward reverence', compels him to take off his cycle-clips, as he would remove his hat in church if he had one. He idly and mockingly reads aloud a few verses from the lectern Bible in the parsonical manner he associates with the place, perhaps surprising and even shocking himself a little as the echoes 'snigger', miming his own facetiousness. The putting of an Irish sixpence in the collection box is an ambivalent action: Larkin has said that the original church which prompted the poem was in Ireland but that the poem takes place in England. The Irish sixpence is of value, but not much and not immediately.

The third stanza begins a process of slightly more serious speculation about the future, though still marked with touches of dismissiveness and a general incomprehension. Belief, he takes it, is already dead; superstition, which he supposes will replace it, will die in its turn. Will only antiquarians and nostalgic sentimentalists find anything here in time to come? He is contemptuous of their interests (underlined in the belittling words: 'the crew/That tap and jot . . .', 'Some ruin-bibber, randy for antique', 'Christmas-addict'). But by the sixth stanza, the supposed future 'representative' of the speaker takes on a dignity imposed by the place and what it stood for: the ordering and ritualising of basic human moments ('marriage, and birth,/And death'), enclosed by these walls. The measured tread of the final stanza establishes this from its first line, and is reinforced by a more ceremonial language – 'blent air', 'compulsions', 'robed as destinies', 'gravitating' (which partly suggests 'gravity', emphasising the repeated 'serious . . . serious . . . serious'). The accumulation of the past, measured by the dead who lie in the churchyard, is the inheritance of the present.

THE TREES. An example of Larkin at his most purely lyrical, beautifully stitched together in three rhyming quatrains. The paradox by which new growth suggests the inevitability of change and death, and the identification of this with human life, is an embodiment of 'something almost being said', of what the trees 'seem to say'. The unobtrusive technical balance is worth noticing: for example, the parallelism of 'trees' and 'leaf' in half-rhyme and of the alliterative 'something . . . said', 'recent . . . relax', 'greenness . . . grief' in the first stanza.

Vernon Scannell

Vernon Scannell was born in 1922. He served in the infantry throughout the Second World War, finally going on the run as a deserter. His wartime experience was important to him, but beyond that his characteristic note is one that is straightforward, colloquial, commonsensical, sometimes tough, but often also wryly aware of the gap between the romantic dream and the debased reality. Scannell has said of his own practice: 'I write about things, people, events in the real world, and I try to do so as honestly as I can, striving to avoid the temptation to fake or posture, to attempt to extract more emotional juice than in fact resides in the situation which is the subject of the poem.' He published *Selected Poems* in 1980.

Dead Dog

One day I found a lost dog in the street.
The hairs about its grin were spiked with blood,
And it lay still as stone. It must have been
A little dog, for though I only stood
Nine inches for each one of my four years
I picked it up and took it home. My mother
Squealed, and later father spaded out
A bed and tucked my mongrel down in mud.

I can't remember any feeling but
A moderate pity, cool not swollen-eyed;
Almost a godlike feeling now it seems.
My lump of dog was ordinary as bread.
I have no recollection of the school
Where I was taught my terror of the dead.

Walking Wounded

A mammoth morning moved grey flanks and groaned.
In the rusty hedges pale rags of mist hung;
The gruel of mud and leaves in the mauled lane
Smelled sweet, like blood. Birds had died or flown,
Their green and silent attics sprouting now
With branches of leafed steel, hiding round eyes
And ripe grenades ready to drop and burst.
In the ditch at the cross-roads the fallen rider lay
Hugging his dead machine and did not stir
At crunch of mortar, tantrum of a Bren
Answering a Spandau's manic jabber.
Then into sight the ambulances came,
Stumbling and churning past the broken farm,
The amputated sign-post and smashed trees,
Slow wagonloads of bandaged cries, square trucks
That rolled on ominous wheels, vehicles
Made mythopoeic by their mortal freight
And crimson crosses on the dirty white.
This grave procession passed, though, for a while,
The grinding of their engines could be heard,
A dark noise on the pallor of the morning,
Dark as dried blood; and then it faded, died.
The road was empty, but it seemed to wait –
Like a stage which knows the cast is in the wings –
Wait for a different traffic to appear.
The mist still hung in snags from dripping thorns;
Absent-minded guns still sighed and thumped.
And then they came, the walking wounded,
Straggling the road like convicts loosely chained,
Dragging at ankles exhaustion and despair.
Their heads were weighted down by last night's lead,
And eyes still drank the dark. They trailed the night
Along the morning road. Some limped on sticks;
Others wore rough dressings, splints and slings;
A few had turbanned heads, the dirty cloth
Brown-badged with blood. A humble brotherhood,

Not one was suffering from a lethal hurt,
They were not magnified by noble wounds,
There was no splendour in that company.
And yet, remembering after eighteen years,
In the heart's throat a sour sadness stirs;
Imagination pauses and returns
To see them walking still, but multiplied
In thousands now. And when heroic corpses
Turn slowly in their decorated sleep
And every ambulance has disappeared
The walking wounded still trudge down that lane,
And when recalled they must bear arms again.

A Case of Murder

They should not have left him there alone,
Alone that is except for the cat.
He was only nine, not old enough
To be left alone in a basement flat,
Alone, that is, except for the cat.
A dog would have been a different thing,
A big gruff dog with slashing jaws,
But a cat with round eyes mad as gold,
Plump as a cushion with tucked-in paws –
Better have left him with a fair-sized rat!
But what they did was leave him with a cat.
He hated that cat; he watched it sit,
A buzzing machine of soft black stuff,
He sat and watched and he hated it,
Snug in its fur, hot blood in a muff,
And its mad gold stare and the way it sat
Crooning dark warmth: he loathed all that.
So he took Daddy's stick and he hit the cat.
Then quick as a sudden crack in glass
It hissed, black flash, to a hiding place

In the dust and dark beneath the couch,
And he followed the grin on his new-made face,
A wide-eyed, frightened snarl of a grin,
And he took the stick and he thrust it in,
Hard and quick in the furry dark.
The black fur squealed and he felt his skin
Prickle with sparks of dry delight.
Then the cat again came into sight,
Shot for the door that wasn't quite shut,
But the boy, quick too, slammed fast the door:
The cat, half-through, was cracked like a nut
And the soft black thud was dumped on the floor.
Then the boy was suddenly terrified
And he bit his knuckles and cried and cried;
But he had to do something with the dead thing there.
His eyes squeezed beads of salty prayer
But the wound of fear gaped wide and raw;
He dared not touch the thing with his hands
So he fetched a spade and shovelled it
And dumped the load of heavy fur
In the spidery cupboard under the stair
Where it's been for years, and though it died
It's grown in that cupboard and its hot low purr
Grows slowly louder year by year:
There'll not be a corner for the boy to hide
When the cupboard swells and all sides split
And the huge black cat pads out of it.

Notes

DEAD DOG. Notice how the monosyllabic simplicity of the first eight lines reinforces the child-like, child-centred anecdote, which is then allowed, in retrospect, the adult judiciousness of 'moderate', 'godlike', 'recollection'.

WALKING WOUNDED. This memory of the Second World War, in which Scannell was on active service in North Africa, Italy and France, carries a great deal of powerful and poignant detail which he manages not to over-play. The weightiness is partly achieved by the steady alliterative tread, each line usually turning on two initial consonants. A final couplet incisively but tenderly rounds off what is otherwise slow-moving blank verse. In what ways does 'Walking Wounded' remind you of Wilfred Owen's First World War poems? Or is it more like Siegfried Sassoon? Or is it unlike either of these?

A CASE OF MURDER. As in 'Dead Dog', and with the same instinctive purposefulness, the monosyllables suggest the boy himself rather than the adult telling the story; and the macabre details are strengthened by this simplicity. Compare (or contrast) this with what Edgar Allan Poe does in his story 'The Tell-Tale Heart' or – most obviously – in 'The Black Cat'.

Patricia Beer

Patricia Beer was born in 1924. She is a poet whose particular gift is for suggesting the doubts and uncertainties which lie just beneath the surface of day-to-day living. In a very good poem, 'Self-Help', she considers the nature of her own progress from a hard-working West Country childhood to where 'now I sit in Hampstead Village/ On a Georgian sofa reading Samuel Smiles/ In paperback . . .' This mixture of plain statement and a rather droll sense of irony is characteristic of her approach, but what gives many of her poems particular force is the manner in which she resolves them. She does not rest comfortably in a sense of irony, as do many lesser poets with her kind of talent, but worries away at something deeper, the sources of her need to achieve an elegant detachment. The closing lines of 'Self-Help' (to be found in her *Selected Poems*, Hutchinson 1979) show this tendency clearly and to great effect: 'And through/ The white comfortable mist a wind blows holes,/ Lays bare the quagmire reaching for us all,/ Whispers how soon we could be shouting "Help".'

After Death

Opening up the house
After three weeks away
I found bird droppings
All over the ground floor,
White and heavy on the windows,
On the worktop,
On the cupboards,
On every wild hope of freedom.

I could not find any bird
At first, and feared
Some science fiction mystery,
To be horribly explained
As soon as whatever
It was felt sure
It had got me alone,
A mile from the village.

At last I discovered him,
Weightless and out of the running,
More null than old wrapping paper
A month after Christmas.
No food inside him, of course,
He had died of hunger
And no waste either,
He was quite empty.

His desperate ghost
Flew down my throat and my ears.
There was no air
He had not suffered in.
He lay in one place,
His droppings were everywhere
More vivid, more terrible
Than he had been, ever.

Prochorus Thompson

Notice Prochorus Thompson. He has won
A competition with the smallest bones
In the whole churchyard. And the man-size grave
He shares with none tops all the tombstones.

Three months of life two hundred years ago.
From harvest time to ailing in November
He came to nothing much, even that Christmas
Not much for anybody to remember.

But little Prochorus Thompson bides his time.
He is the right length for sight-seers
Who pay no attention to the corpses
That lived for fifty, sixty speaking years.

Evergreen and rank are the paths between
The yew trees, and lichen creeps like evil
Over men who worked hard and dropped dead,
Women at menopause who saw the devil.

The balance of the churchyard must be righted.
May the full-grown dead seem interesting. May all
Children live longer than Prochorus Thompson.
Strangle the church tower and the passing bell.

Arms

I was brought up to believe
In the Everlasting Arms
And took comfort for some years
In the fatherly muscle
And grip, but fell out of them
Gradually and in slow
Motion as God dissolved. Fell
Into nightmares about arms

And specially one picture
Of the world lying flooded
With all the animals drowned,
Visible still in one foot
Of water, frozen, never
To wriggle with the tide or
Rustle to pieces. Stiff-legged
The sheep who could not embrace

And flex as the lions could
Nevertheless lay in their
Ramrod protectiveness
Holding each other like bars.
These limbs were not immortal
And, perishing, they woke me
As in a story I heard:
When my grandfather went down

With his brig in the North Sea
On a calm clear evening
There was no wireless to send
Last love on. He put his arms
Round his son and there he stood,
Protector, up to his knees
In death, and that was the last
That anyone saw of him.

Notes

AFTER DEATH. This deceptively simple poem moves with an unobtrusive but firm artistry from its low-key, anecdotal beginning towards a chilly, memorable final stanza. It enlarges a small event into an occasion of striking tenderness and horror. Worth careful attention is the manner in which the conversational tone is used to create both anticipation and emphasis; how, for example, at the end, the placing of 'ever' seems to carry the maximum emotional weight. One might consider what would be lost if the last two words were reversed.

PROCHORUS THOMPSON. The manner in which the poem moves through gentle irony towards a statement of personal feeling is characteristic of Patricia Beer's poetry. The effects are subtle, and it is often rewarding to dwell on an apparently plain statement which may turn out to carry more weight than is at first noticed. The phrase 'the right length' (verse 3), for example, obviously refers to Prochorus Thompson's size but in a poem about time, history and the itinerary of sightseers it can also be felt to have rich *temporal* connotations. It was particularly common in eighteenth and nineteenth century rural England, where religion had a strong hold, to name children after obscure figures from the Bible. Prochorus can be found in Acts 6:5. The passing bell is the bell which sounds at the time of death. An interesting comparison might be made between this poem and John Crowe Ransom's 'The Dead Boy'.

ARMS. The Everlasting Arms are the arms of God the Father, who is depicted here as steadfastly parental. The poem draws on Patricia Beer's upbringing in a family of Plymouth Brethren (see her prose autobiography *Mrs Beer's House*) and the biblical picture described has all the character of the powerfully direct illustrations to be found in popular religious literature of the nineteenth century. In this case the subject is the Flood, and it acts as an imaginative transition between the loss of religious conviction acknowledged in the first verse and the plain, resonant emphasis on human tenderness and mortality in the last. The poem is written in syllabics (seven-syllable lines throughout.

Peter Porter

Peter Porter was born in Australia in 1929, but has lived in England since 1951. When some of his first poems started to appear in the early 1960s, he seemed to be primarily a satirist of contemporary life (as he himself put it, 'a wielder of brand names and journalistic tags'). His work as an advertising copywriter at that time was (quite wrongly) enough for some people to condemn him as smart and superficial. Porter can certainly catch the tone of voice of several kinds of modern rhetoric (in their different ways in 'A Consumer's Report' and 'Mort aux Chats'); but increasingly he has become a richly various elegiac poet, sometimes grandly stately, sometimes cryptic and oblique, ranging across a wide area of history, art, and human experience. He is one of the most inventive and entertaining poets now writing. He has published nine books of poems, but not yet a collected volume. The most recent are *The Cost of Seriousness* (1978) and *English Subtitles* (1981).

A Consumer's Report

The name of the product I tested is *Life*,
I have completed the form you sent me
and understand that my answers are confidential.

I had it as a gift,
I didn't feel much while using it,
in fact I think I'd have liked to be more excited.
It seemed gentle on the hands
but left an embarrassing deposit behind.
It was not economical
and I have used much more than I thought
(I suppose I have about half left
but it's difficult to tell) –
although the instructions are fairly large
there are so many of them
I don't know which to follow, especially
as they seem to contradict each other.
I'm not sure such a thing
should be put in the way of children –
It's difficult to think of a purpose
for it. One of my friends says
it's just to keep its maker in a job.
Also the price is much too high.
Things are piling up so fast,
after all, the world got by
for a thousand million years
without this, do we need it now?
(Incidentally, please ask your man
to stop calling me 'the respondent',
I don't like the sound of it.)
There seems to be a lot of different labels,
sizes and colours should be uniform,
the shape is awkward, it's waterproof
but not heat resistant, it doesn't keep
yet it's very difficult to get rid of:
whenever they make it cheaper they seem

to put less in — if you say you don't
want it, then it's delivered anyway.
I'd agree it's a popular product,
it's got into the language; people
even say they're on the side of it.
Personally I think it's overdone,
a small thing people are ready
to behave badly about. I think
we should take it for granted. If its
experts are called philosophers or market
researchers or historians, we shouldn't
care. We are the consumers and the last
law makers. So finally, I'd buy it.
But the question of a 'best buy'
I'd like to leave until I get
the competitive product you said you'd send.

Mort aux Chats

There will be no more cats.
Cats spread infection,
cats pollute the air,
cats consume seven times
their own weight in food a week,
cats were worshipped in
decadent societies (Egypt
and Ancient Rome), the Greeks
had no use for cats. Cats
sit down to pee (our scientists
have proved it.) The copulation
of cats is harrowing; they
are unbearably fond of the moon.
Perhaps they are all right in
their own country but their
traditions are alien to ours.

Cats smell, they can't help it,
you notice it going upstairs.
Cats watch too much television,
they can sleep through storms,
they stabbed us in the back
last time. There have never been
any great artists who were cats.
They don't deserve a capital C
except at the beginning of a sentence.
I blame my headache and my
plants dying on to cats.
Our district is full of them,
property values are falling.
When I dream of God I see
a Massacre of Cats. Why
should they insist on their own
language and religion, who
needs to purr to make his point?
Death to all cats! The Rule
of Dogs shall last a thousand years!

May, 1945

As the Allied tanks trod Germany to shard
and no man had seen a fresh-pressed uniform
for six months, as the fire storm
bit out the core of Dresden yard by yard,

as farmers hid turnips for the after-war,
as cadets going to die passed Waffen SS
tearing identifications from their battledress,
the Russians only three days from the Brandenburger Tor –

in the very hell of sticks and blood and brick dust
as Germany the phoenix burned, the wraith
of History pursed its lips and spoke, thus:

To go with teeth and toes and human soap,
the radio will broadcast Bruckner's Eighth
so that good and evil may die in equal hope.

An Angel in Blythburgh Church

Shot down from its enskied formation,
This stern-faced plummet rests against the wall;
Cromwell's soldiers peppered it and now the death-
    watch beetle has it in thrall.

If you make fortunes from wool, along
The weeping winter foreshores of the tide,
You build big churches with clerestories
    And place angels high inside.

Their painted faces guard and guide. Now or
Tomorrow or whenever is the promise –
The resurrection comes: fix your eyes halfway
    Between Heaven and Diss.

The face is crudely carved, simplified by wind;
It looks straight at God and waits for orders,
Buffeted by the organ militant, and blasted
    By choristers and recorders.

Faith would have our eyes as wooden and as certain.
It might be worth it, to start the New Year's hymn
Allowing for death as a mere calculation,
    A depreciation, entered in.

Or so I fancy looking at the roof beams
Where the dangerous beetle sails. What is it
Turns an atheist's mind to prayer in almost
    Any church on a country visit?

Greed for love or certainty or forgiveness?
High security rising with the sea birds?
A theology of self looking for precedents?
A chance to speak old words?

Rather, I think of a woman lying on her bed
Staring for hours up to the ceiling where
Nothing is projected – death the only angel
To shield her from despair.

Notes

A CONSUMER'S REPORT. Porter worked for several years in an advertising agency, and has occasionally drawn on this for themes and images. This poem among other things parodies the questions and responses contained in the kind of report on which manufacturers and advertisers rely when they are testing the public's response to a product, whether it is soap, cigarettes, or whatever else. What is 'Life' as a product? And is 'the competitive product' Death?

MORT AUX CHATS. This is one of two poems Porter published together with the title 'Two Poems with French Titles'. 'Mort aux Chats' ('Death to Cats') he took as a title from a painting by the artist Louis Wain, whose speciality was comic or whimsical pictures of cats. The poem itself is written as an amusing essay in rhetoric – the rhetoric of prejudice, whereby strong feelings are based on misinformation, ignorance, intolerance, fear and hatred. Many of the criticisms of cats are of course transpositions of remarks made about Jews, non-white people, and indeed any minority, nationality or religious persuasion which has been (or is) felt by some to be dangerous, hostile, or inferior. It was said by Churchill of the Italians, when they entered the war as allies of Nazi Germany in 1940, that they had stabbed us in the back. Hitler said of his Third Reich that it would last a thousand years.

MAY, 1945. This grim sonnet reconstructs the final days of the Second World War in Europe, with Nazi Germany on the point of collapse: the city of Dresden had been almost entirely destroyed by Allied fire bombing, and Berlin (where the Brandenburger Tor is) was about to be entered by Soviet troops. During these days, the German radio broadcast much solemn music – including Bruckner's Eighth Symphony – as if it were indeed the funeral of a nation. Alongside this destruction and the reconciliation of sublime art at such a moment, Porter sets the 'teeth and toes and human soap' of the Nazi concentration camps, which were being discovered with horror by the Allied forces at the same time.

AN ANGEL IN BLYTHBURGH CHURCH. The huge parish church at Blythburgh in Suffolk, built at a time when East Anglia was rich with the profits from wool, has a magnificent series of carved wooden angels looking down from the roof of the nave. One of them ('This stern-faced plummet') has been taken down and placed against the wall by a window. Diss (a town on the Norfolk-Suffolk border not far away) sounds uncomfortably like *Dis*, the Roman hell. In the poem, the certitudes of faith are balanced ironically against not just agnosticism or atheism but against despair.

Thom Gunn

Thom Gunn was born in 1929 and educated in Cambridge where he first came to attention as a poet while still at the University. For some years now, however, he has been living on the coast of California where the landscape and the social patterns – particularly those of youth culture – have appealed to him greatly, becoming an important theme in his poetry. But whatever his immediate subject is, his underlying concerns are with the sources of action and the process of observation. In the poems with which he made his name – 'clenched', to use his own description of them, and hard-edged – he attempts to define the tension between opposites: rule and energy, will and instinct, intellectual rigour and the modes of pleasure. Of these, 'On the Move' (included here) is a good example. Since he has increasingly come to be interested in the use of syllabics as well as the iambic metre and tightly rhymed stanza, a gentler note has entered his poetry, and his much advertised toughness has become balanced by an almost benign strain of celebration. His *Selected Poems* were published by Faber and Faber in 1979.

On the Move

The blue jay scuffling in the bushes follows
Some hidden purpose, and the gust of birds
That spurts across the field, the wheeling swallows,
Have nested in the trees and undergrowth.
Seeking their instinct, or their poise, or both,
One moves with an uncertain violence
Under the dust thrown by a baffled sense
Or the dull thunder of approximate words.

On motorcycles, up the road, they come:
Small, black, as flies hanging in heat, the Boys,
Until the distance throws them forth, their hum
Bulges to thunder held by calf and thigh.
In goggles, donned impersonality,
In gleaming jackets trophied with the dust,
They strap in doubt — by hiding it, robust —
And almost hear a meaning in their noise.

Exact conclusion of their hardiness
Has no shape yet, but from known whereabouts
They ride, direction where the tires press.
They scare a flight of birds across the field:
Much that is natural, to the will must yield.
Men manufacture both machine and soul,
And use what they imperfectly control
To dare a future from the taken routes.

It is a part solution, after all.
One is not necessarily discord
On earth; or damned because, half animal,
One lacks direct instinct, because one wakes
Afloat on movement that divides and breaks.
One joins the movement in a valueless world,
Choosing it, till, both hurler and the hurled,
One moves as well, always toward, toward.

A minute holds them, who have come to go:
The self-defined, astride the created will
They burst away; the towns they travel through
Are home for neither bird nor holiness,
For birds and saints complete their purposes.
At worst, one is in motion; and at best,
Reaching no absolute, in which to rest,
One is always nearer by not keeping still.

Innocence

(to Tony White)

He ran the course and as he ran he grew,
And smelt his fragrance in the field. Already,
Running he knew the most he ever knew,
The egotism of a healthy body.

Ran into manhood, ignorant of the past:
Culture of guilt and guilt's vague heritage,
Self-pity and the soul; what he possessed
Was rich, potential, like the bud's tipped rage.

The Corps developed, it was plain to see,
Courage, endurance, loyalty and skill
To a morale firm as morality,
Hardening him to an instrument, until

The finitude of virtues that were there
Bodied within the swarthy uniform
A compact innocence, child-like and clear,
No doubt could penetrate, no act could harm.

When he stood near the Russian partisan
Being burned alive, he therefore could behold
The ribs wear gently through the darkening skin
And sicken only at the Northern cold,

Could watch the fat burn with a violet flame
And feel disgusted only at the smell,
And judge that all pain finishes the same
As melting quietly by his boots it fell.

The Fair in the Woods

(to Jere Fransway)

The woodsmen blow their horns, and close the day,
Grouped by some logs. The buckskins they are in
Merge with ground's russet and with tree-trunk's grey,
And through the colour of the body's skin
Shift borrowings out of nearby birch and clay.

All day a mounted angel came and went
Sturdily pacing through the trees and crowd,
His horse glossy and obedient.
Points glowed among his hair: dark-haired, dark-browed.
He supervised a god's experiment.

Some clustered in the upper boughs, from where
They watched the groups beneath them make their way,
Children of light, all different, through the fair,
Pulsing among the pulsing trunks. And they,
The danglers, ripened in the brilliant air.

Upon a platform dappled by the sun
The whole speed-family in a half round clapped
About the dancer where she arched and spun.
They raced toward stillness till they overlapped,
Ten energies working inward through the one.

Landscape of acid:
    where on fern and mound
The lights fragmented by the roofing bough
Throbbed outward, joining over broken ground
To one long dazzling burst; as even now
Horn closes over horn into one sound.

Knuckle takes back its colour, nail its line.
Slowly the tawny jerkins separate
From bark and earth, but they will recombine
In the autumnal dusk, for it is late.
The horns call. There is little left to shine.

LSD, San Rafael Woods: 'Renaissance Fair'

Back to Life

Around the little park
The lamps blink on, and make the dusk seem deeper.
I saunter toward them on the grass
That suddenly rustles from the dew,
Hearing behind, at times,
A fragmentary shout or distant bark.
I am alone, like a patrolling keeper.
And then I catch the smell of limes
Coming and going faintly on the dark:
Bunched black at equal height
They stand between the lamps, yet where
They branch out toward them on each side, a few
Touching the lighted glass,
Their leaves are soft green on the night,
The closest losing even their mass,
Edged but transparent as if they too gave light.

The street is full, the quiet is broken.
I notice that the other strollers there
Extend themselves, at ease
As if just woken
To a world they have not yet recovered, though
They move across the dusk, alert,
And stare,
As I do, into shops or at the trees,

112

Devouring each detail, from leaf to dirt,
In the measured mildness of the air.
Here by the kerb
The boys and girls walk, jostling as they grow,
Cocky with surplus strength.
And weakening with each move, the old,
Cushioned with papers or with rugs
On public seats close by,
Inch down into their loosened flesh, each fold
Being sensible of the gravity
Which tugs
And longs to bring it down
And break its hold.

I walk between the kerb and bench
Conscious at length
Of sharing through each sense,
As if the light revealed us all
Sustained in delicate difference
Yet firmly growing from a single branch.

If that were all of it!
The branch that we grow on
Is not remembered easily in the dark,
Or the transparency when light is gone:
At most, a recollection
In the mind only – over a rainswept park
Held to by mere conviction
In cold and misery when the clock strikes one.

The lamp still shines.
The pale leaves shift a bit,
Now light, now shadowed, and their movement shared
A second later by the bough,
Even by the sap that runs through it:
A small full trembling through it now
As if each leaf were, so, better prepared
For falling sooner or later separate.

The Discovery of the Pacific

They lean against the cooling car, backs pressed
Upon the dusts of a brown continent,
And watch the sun, now Westward of their West,
Fall to the ocean. Where it led they went.

Kansas to California. Day by day
They travelled emptier of the things they knew.
They improvised new habits on the way,
But lost the occasions, and then lost them too.

One night, no-one and nowhere, she had woken
To resin-smell and to the firs' slight sound,
And through their sleeping-bag had felt the broken
Tight-knotted surfaces of the naked ground.

Only his lean quiet body cupping hers
Kept her from it, the extreme chill. By degrees
She fell asleep. Around them in the firs
The wind probed, tiding through forked estuaries.

And now their skin is caked with road, the grime
Merely reflecting sunlight as it fails.
They leave their clothes among the rocks they climb,
Blunt leaves of iceplant nuzzle at their soles.

Now they stand chin-deep in the sway of ocean,
Firm West, two stringy bodies face to face,
And come, together, in the water's motion,
The full caught pause of their embrace.

Last Days at Teddington

The windows wide through day and night
Gave on the garden like a room.
The garden smell, green composite,
Flowed in and out a house in bloom.

To the shaggy dog who skidded from
The concrete through the kitchen door
To yellow-squared linoleum,
It was an undivided floor.

How green it was indoors. The thin
Pale creepers climbed up brick until
We saw their rolled tongues flicker in
Across the cracked paint of the sill.

How sociable the garden was.
We ate and talked in given light.
The children put their toys to grass
All the warm wakeful August night.

So coming back from drinking late
We picked our way below the wall
But in the higher grass, dewed wet,
Stumbled on tricycle and ball.

When everything was moved away,
The house returned to board and shelf,
And smelt of hot dust through the day,
The garden fell back on itself.

Notes

ON THE MOVE. The leather-jacketed boys riding apparently aimlessly from one place to another on their motorcycles take on a strange authority as the poem pursues its argument. Throughout the poem, instinctiveness and fluidity are defined in a changing number of ways, from the blue jay and the swallows of the first stanza, whose purpose is 'hidden', or the boys whose restless movement 'lacks direct instinct', to a fusion of instinct and will which joins them. Restlessness, the refusal to settle on an 'absolute', is endorsed as a means towards purpose and harmony 'in a valueless world' ('valueless' in the sense of 'without accepted values'.)

The tightly organised stanza form helps to give an authoritative stamp to ideas which are tentative rather than dogmatic: it is not only the boys' doubt that is being strapped in, and one should notice the limiting force of 'almost' in 'And almost hear a meaning in their noise'. (Compare 'Our almost-instinct almost true' in Philip Larkin's 'An Arundel Tomb'.)

Behind the whole poem there stands a potent image of the 1950s, when it was written: gangs of anarchic youths in leather jackets on motorcycles roaring through the American countryside and cities, as in Marlon Brando's film *The Wild Ones*. Behind it, too, is an acquaintance with Sartre's notion of existential freedom, with its emphasis on the individual taking risks.

INNOCENCE. There is a flat matter-of-factness about the way this poem proceeds, as rigidly boxed-in as the doctrine which created the Nazi SS man about whom it is written. The first four stanzas are 'plain to see', presenting an 'innocence' grounded in ignorance (of the past and the inheritance of the past, religion and religious notions grounded in guilt). The man has been hardened 'to an instrument'; and the hardening has resulted not only in toughness but callousness, a disregard of pain in others as in oneself. The fifth and sixth stanzas narrow down to an extreme example of this callousness, still controlled by the undemonstrative *abab* quatrains but made the more shockingly vivid by the physical details – the partisan's ribs, the look and smell of the burning flesh. The three conjunctions – 'and sicken

116

. . . and feel . . . and judge' – coldly emphasise the inevitability of the process. Throughout the poem, no overt judgement is made.

THE FAIR IN THE WOODS. The collection in which this poem first appears is *Moly* (1971). Moly was a mythological herb (mentioned in Homer's *Odyssey*) endowed with magic properties – 'cool flesh of magic in each leaf and shoot/ From milky flower to the black forked root' as Gunn describes it in the volume's title poem – and a number of the poems are concerned with drugs. The documentary note at the end of 'The Fair in the Woods' indicates that the poem was written after using LSD (lysergic acid), as is plain enough both from the entire contents, its intense visual glow, and several specific references. 'Speed' and 'acid' are common names for LSD. By a subtle process of description, Gunn interweaves the details of a mythological sylvan scene and a contemporary festival: the horns and the dancer are at once part of a legendary pastoral and a modern rock group. Even the 'mounted angel' on his 'glossy horse' is, presumably, a Hell's Angel on his motorbike.

BACK TO LIFE. The lines 'Devouring each detail, from leaf to dirt,/ In the measured mildness of the air' (stanza 2) might offer a good starting point for considering this intensely observant and meditative poem. Like much of Gunn's strongest work it draws its strength from the recognition of tensions: here, between body and mind, weight and weightlessness, darkness and light, isolation and community. It also shows the unobtrusive skill with which Gunn arranges his lines of free verse; for example, in the isolated, weighty 'Which tugs' (stanza 2) where the gravity described is demonstrated rhythmically.

THE DISCOVERY OF THE PACIFIC. This poem is set in California where Gunn has lived for most of his writing life. The journey described is at the same time a physical move from Kansas to California and a metaphorical quest for consummation and peace. This gives a particular edge to the title. 'Pacific' may be read both in its geographical sense and as indicating the state of (tending towards) peace. The 'iceplant' (stanza 5) is a succulent, thick-leaved plant which flourishes in sandy soil. Notice how the verb 'nuzzle', with its associations of gentleness and affection, prepares for the embrace with which the poem ends.

LAST DAYS AT TEDDINGTON. The benign English setting is beautifully captured by the relaxed iambic tetrameters and precise, though unconstraining, quatrains. One senses that the whole poem, with its underlying vision of a tamed wilderness, is gratefully received and generously given, like the light in stanza 4. It might not be too fanciful to suggest that what gives the poem its particular poignancy is the fact that the recollections are indeed of 'last days' and that a kind of idealised domestic paradise is now viewed from the distance of 'exile'.

Ted Hughes

Ted Hughes was born in 1930. When in 1956 his first collection, *The Hawk in the Rain*, received a First Publication Award from the New York Poetry Center, one of the judges, Marianne Moore, noted how the poems were 'aglow with feeling'; and when the book appeared in this country another distinguished poet of an older generation, Edwin Muir, wrote: 'His distinguishing power is sensuous, verbal and imaginative: at his best the three are fused together. His images have an admirable violence.' Certainly violence has remained of the essence in Hughes's work, embodied in an urgent rhythmic force, a fierce vocabulary and an elemental subject matter, but whether or not it is always admirable is open to serious question. Since the publication of *Crow* (Faber and Faber, 1970) Hughes's immense energy has often seemed to be flailing and indulging itself in a vacuum, the violence becoming a series of crude captions which bludgeon the reader into insensitivity rather than engaging the imagination. The word 'demonic' has entered critical discussion of his work, defining the quality which has loomed between his admirers and detractors. At the same time, however, a more controlled and subtle imagination has persisted in much of his admirable poetry for younger readers and, outstandingly, in the first section of his recent collection *Moortown* (1979).

Hawk Roosting

I sit in the top of the wood, my eyes closed.
Inaction, no falsifying dream
Between my hooked head and hooked feet:
Or in sleep rehearse perfect kills and eat.

The convenience of the high trees!
The air's buoyancy and the sun's ray
Are of advantage to me;
And the earth's face upward for my inspection.

My feet are locked upon the rough bark.
It took the whole of Creation
To produce my foot, my each feather:
Now I hold Creation in my foot

Or fly up, and revolve it all slowly –
I kill where I please because it is all mine.
There is no sophistry in my body:
My manners are tearing off heads –

The allotment of death.
For the one path of my flight is direct
Through the bones of the living.
No arguments assert my right:

The sun is behind me.
Nothing has changed since I began.
My eye has permitted no change.
I am going to keep things like this.

Thistles

Against the rubber tongues of cows and the hoeing hands of
    men
Thistles spike the summer air
Or crackle open under a blue-black pressure.

Every one a revengeful burst
Of resurrection, a grasped fistful
Of splintered weapons and Icelandic frost thrust up

From the underground stain of a decayed Viking.
They are like pale hair and the gutturals of dialects.
Every one manages a plume of blood.

Then they grow grey, like men.
Mown down, it is a feud. Their sons appear,
Stiff with weapons, fighting back over the same ground.

Full Moon and Little Frieda

A cool small evening shrunk to a dog bark and the clank of a
    bucket –

And you listening.
A spider's web, tense for the dew's touch.
A pail lifted, still and brimming – mirror
To tempt a first star to a tremor.

Cows are going home in the lane there, looping the hedges
        with their warm wreaths of breath –
A dark river of blood, many boulders,
Balancing unspilled milk.

'Moon!' you cry suddenly, 'Moon! Moon!'

The moon has stepped back like an artist gazing amazed at a
    work
That points at him amazed.

Crow Goes Hunting

Crow
Decided to try words.

He imagined some words for the job, a lovely pack –
Clear-eyed, resounding, well-trained,
With strong teeth.
You could not find a better bred lot.

He pointed out the hare and away went the words
Resounding.
Crow was Crow without fail, but what is a hare?

It converted itself to a concrete bunker.
The words circled protesting, resounding.

Crow turned the words into bombs – they blasted the bunker.
The bits of bunker flew up – a flock of starlings.

Crow turned the words into shotguns, they shot down the
    starlings.
The falling starlings turned to a cloudburst.

Crow turned the words into a reservoir, collecting the water.
The water turned into an earthquake, swallowing the reservoir.

The earthquake turned into a hare and leaped for the hill
Having eaten Crow's words.

Crow gazed after the bounding hare
Speechless with admiration.

A Childish Prank

Man's and woman's bodies lay without souls,
Dully gaping, foolishly staring, inert
On the flowers of Eden.
God pondered.

The problem was so great, it dragged him asleep.

Crow laughed.
He bit the Worm, God's only son,
Into two writhing halves.

He stuffed into man the tail half
With the wounded end hanging out.

He stuffed the head half headfirst into woman
And it crept in deeper and up
To peer out through her eyes
Calling its tail-half to join up quickly, quickly
Because O it was painful.

Man awoke being dragged across the grass.
Woman awoke to see him coming.
Neither knew what had happened.

God went on sleeping.

Crow went on laughing.

His Legs Ran About

Till they tangled and seemed to trip and lie down
With her legs intending to hold them there forever

His arms lifted things, groped in dark rooms, at last with their
    hands
Caught her arms
And lay down enwoven at last at last

Mouth talked its way in and out and finally
Found her mouth and settled deeper deeper

His chest pushed until it came up against
Her breast at the end of everything

His navel fitted over her navel as closely as possible
Like a mirror face down flat on a mirror

And so when every part
Like a bull pushing towards its cows, not to be stayed
Like a calf seeking its mama
Like a desert staggerer, among his hallucinations
Seeking the hoof-churned hole

Finally got what it needed, and grew still, and closed its eyes

Then such greatness and truth descended

As over a new grave, when the mourners have gone
And the stars come out
And the earth, bristling and raw, tiny and lost,
Resumes its search

Rushing through the vast astonishment.

The Stag

While the rain fell on the November woodland shoulder of
   Exmoor
While the traffic jam along the road honked and shouted
Because the farmers were parking wherever they could
And scrambling to the bank-top to stare through the tree-fringe
Which was leafless,
The stag ran through his private forest.

While the rain drummed on the roofs of the parked cars
And the kids inside cried and daubed their chocolate and fought
And mothers and aunts and grandmothers
Were a tangle of undoing sandwiches and screwed-round
   gossiping heads
Steaming up the windows,
The stag loped through his favourite valley.

While the blue horsemen down in the boggy meadow
Sodden nearly black, on sodden horses,
Spaced as at a military parade,
Moved a few paces to the right and a few to the left and felt
   rather foolish
Looking at the brown impassable river,
The stag came over the last hill of Exmoor.

While everybody high-kneed it to the bank-top all along the
   road
Where steady men in oilskins were stationed at binoculars,
And the horsemen by the river galloped anxiously this way and
   that
And the cry of hounds came tumbling invisibly with their
   echoes down through the draggle of trees,
Swinging across the wall of dark woodland,
The stag dropped into a strange country.

And turned at the river

Hearing the hound-pack smash the undergrowth, hearing the
    bell-note

Of the voice that carried all the others,

Then while his limbs all cried different directions to his lungs,
    which only wanted to rest,

The blue horsemen on the bank opposite

Pulled aside the camouflage of their terrible planet.

And the stag doubled back weeping and looking for home up a
    valley and down a valley

While the strange trees struck at him and the brambles lashed
    him,

And the strange earth came galloping after him carrying the
    loll-tongued hounds to fling all over him

And his heart became just a club beating his ribs and his own
    hooves shouted with hounds' voices,

And the crowd on the road got back into their cars

Wet-through and disappointed.

Coming Down Through Somerset

I flash-glimpsed in the headlights – the high moment
Of driving through England – a killed badger
Sprawled with helpless legs. Yet again
Manoeuvred lane-ends, retracked, waited
Out of decency for headlights to die,
Lifted by one warm hindleg in the world-night
A slain badger. August dust-heat. Beautiful,
Beautiful, warm, secret beast. Bedded him
Passenger, bleeding from the nose. Brought him close
Into my life. Now he lies on the beam
Torn from a great building. Beam waiting two years
To be built into new building. Summer coat
Not worth skinning off him. His skeleton – for the future.

Fangs, handsome concealed. Flies, drumming,
Bejewel his transit. Heatwave ushers him hourly
Towards his underworlds. A grim day of flies
And sunbathing. Get rid of that badger.
A night of shrunk rivers, glowing pastures,
Sea-trout shouldering up through trickles. Then the sun again
Waking like a torn-out eye. How strangely
He stays on into the dawn — how quiet
The dark bear-claws, the long frost-tipped guard hairs!
Get rid of that badger today.
And already the flies,
More passionate, bringing their friends. I don't want
To bury and waste him. Or skin him (it is too late).
Or hack off his head and boil it
To liberate his masterpiece skull. I want him
To stay as he is. Sooty gloss-throated,
With his perfect face. Paws so tired,
Power-body relegated. I want him
To stop time. His strength staying, bulky,
Blocking time. His rankness, his bristling wildness,
His thrilling painted face.
A badger on my moment of life.
Not years ago, like the others, but now.
I stand
Watching his stillness, like an iron nail
Driven, flush to the head,
Into a yew post. Something
Has to stay.

Notes

HAWK ROOSTING. Unlike 'The Thought-Fox', 'Pike', etc., 'Hawk Roosting' is a piece of re-creation from within: the poem is a monologue of the creature itself, which captures its prey as Hughes sees himself capturing a poem. It is also one of the clearest statements Hughes has made on one of his habitual themes: that the instinctive life, or the life of Nature, is something that we have discarded at great cost. In an interview published in 1971, Hughes said of 'Hawk Roosting': 'That bird is accused of being a fascist . . . the symbol of some horrible totalitarian genocidal dictator. Actually what I had in mind was that in this hawk Nature is thinking. Simply Nature.' The implication is that Nature, though ruthless, is at least without 'sophistry' – the clever hypocrisies, deceptions and self-deceptions practised by Man.

THISTLES. This is a fine example (from *Wodwo*) of Hughes using a concentrated cluster of metaphors to show relationships. The tough resilience of thistles is demonstrated by making indirect comparisons between them and warrior Vikings – their sharp weapons, helmets, feuds, even their ancestral handing-on of hair-colour and dialect words. The presence of the Vikings can still be felt in Hughes's home territory of Yorkshire, surviving alongside the thistles.

FULL MOON AND LITTLE FRIEDA. A short, richly atmospheric poem in which small details of observation provide a setting which is both exact and numinous. The sense of wonder experienced by the girl, Hughes's daughter, and the poet's own sense of the moon's splendour are combined in the choice of the word 'amazed'. The subtle way in which this beautifully judged word is repeated within the poem's closing cadence with a gentle but firm stress at the end of the last line suggests a mysterious bond between the child and the moon. The poem also provides an object lesson in the unobtrusive use of alliteration: the sound of the consonants contributes much to the delicate tension set up from the very first line.

CROW GOES HUNTING and A CHILDISH PRANK. The publication of Ted Hughes's *Crow* in 1970 was something of a literary phenomenon. Like many works of undeniable force and originality, it divided the critics. For some, it was an achievement of the first order, a successful attempt to create a myth for our times, while others found it to be a violent hotch-potch of pretentiousness and cliché, a two-dimensional cosmic comic-strip which came far too close to the world of ASTOUNDING enterprises. Whatever the reaction, however, it was a compelling work by a respected poet and thus demanded serious attention. Perhaps the liveliest introduction to it is to be found in Jonathan Raban's *The Society of the Poem* (Harrap 1971), a book which might well be of considerable value to readers of this anthology in that it deals most intelligently with a number of the poets we have included. Raban's account of *Crow's* initial impression is worth quoting here since it is informative as well as a good indication of his succinct and readable approach. Hughes

> appears, in fact, to have reinvented a language for himself, drawn partly from folk-tales, partly from the rhythms and vocabulary of Yorkshire dialect, partly from mythology and epic literature, which has the cold, unsocial force of stone. Crow, the central figure and voice of the series, is the kind of super-bird one might encounter in a horror comic written by John Milton: black, primeval, Adamic; whose power is vested somewhere between the sharpness of his talons and the cosmic irony of his laughter; whose entire being is concentrated into the terrifying, solipsistic art of sheer survival.

Whatever one's reservations, *Crow* is a tour-de-force and should be read as a complete sequence. Of the two poems selected here, 'Crow Goes Hunting' demonstrates Ted Hughes's method of effecting Protean transformations, a technique similar to that used by a number of artists in the field of animated cartoons, and particularly by those East European cartoonists who find it a convenient means of making powerful (though necessarily oblique) political comment: for example, 'Crow turned the words into bombs – they blasted the bunker./ The bits of bunker flew up – a flock of starlings.' This method can also be found in a number of poets from the same region, notably the Czechoslovakian Miroslav Holub and the Yugoslavian Vasko Popa, both of whom Ted Hughes has helped to introduce to English readers.

129

'A Childish Prank' rewrites the story of the Creation in terms of what another poet, Tony Harrison, has described as Crow's 'sorcerer's apprentice relationship with a bungling, comatose God'.

HIS LEGS RAN ABOUT. Although this poem eventually found its place as part of another mythological sequence, *Cave Birds*, it was first published (and even anthologised) separately. Its combination of the grotesque and the lyrical, its list of similes building up to a final resonant statement, is characteristic of Hughes. It is a kind of verse which teeters on the brink of sensationalism but – at its best, as here – kindles and persuades the imagination.

THE STAG, COMING DOWN THROUGH SOMERSET. For some years now Ted Hughes has lived in Devonshire, where he farms, and recently much of his best descriptive work has reflected his close involvement with the local rituals of a rural community and his response to the surrounding landscape. 'The Stag' is taken from his collection of poems for children, *Season Songs* (1976), and 'Coming Down Through Somerset', though it first appeared in a further series for children, has since become part of Hughes's impressive record – almost a verse diary – of farming experience in *Moortown* (1979). Notice the way in which this second poem incorporates both rhetorical repetition and a telegrammatic urgency. A packing together of notebook observation and memoranda ('get rid of that badger') creates a dramatic whole which captures the *awe* that was clearly the poem's source. It is interesting to compare 'Coming Down Through Somerset' with 'Pike', considering the differences in style and organisation of material.

Alan Brownjohn

Alan Brownjohn was born in 1931. Though he began to publish poems while he was still an Oxford undergraduate, Brownjohn has been a slow but steady developer, and his most recent books have been his best: *Warrior's Career* (1972), *A Song of Good Life* (1975) and *A Night in the Gazebo* (1980). Some of the poems in these books have been satirical vignettes (such as 'Warmth', represented here), others have been strange self-contained fictions. One of Brownjohn's strengths is his ability to think his way through his position as what he has called 'a wry kind of English puritan', extending beyond the personal to the social, yet almost always in an approachable and humane way.

Warmth

What made her decide she'd
enjoy being a wee-hours disc-jockey,
well it was something about *giving*
to ordinary people, and well . . . . And
did she like the life now (and how!)
she was part of it, yes she thought
it was a great life, what did she
especially like about it, providing the
sweet music between the News
bulletins, what made it a good life
for *her*? Well, maybe, like she said,
she felt she was doing something
for people. But switching this
round, what was it people did for
her? Well, people were quite
wonderful to her, she couldn't
describe it, it was a kind-of warmth,

you know, coming over to you from
people. As to being the most
popular girl in England to phone in
to, she could only say, giggling
shyly, she loved talking to people,
and though you did get those who,
well, just couldn't get *over* to you,
well, most of the time, you know, the
kind-of warmth, she thought it was just
great. Would she sum it all up, then,
in the same kind-of thing, the kind-of
warmth she felt? Yes, she couldn't
describe it exactly, but it was maybe
just that thing, a kind of . . . warmth
she got from nothing else.

Texas Book Depository

I am writing my text-book of modern American history
It will sell in all the schools
Every school will buy fifty dozen copies
One for every child in every class
In a given year
It should appear about 1963
My book will sell in millions
To the school authorities
It will be stored ready
In millions
On the shelves of great depositories full
Of textbooks for schools
My book will make me a fortune
It will have fine clear diagrams
Fine clear expositions
And be a fine text-book yes
The depositories will be full of it

The depositories will be air-conditioned
Men will walk around the depositories in grey coats
Counting and packaging the books
Including my book
They are wonderful places depositories why
You could get lost in depositories or hide
And not be seen for hours
You will be able to get lost even among the copies
Of my book
I will have done a humble service
Publishing my book
I shall be able to say to myself
I could have done innumerable worse things
Than publishing my book
Than helping to fill with books like mine
Depositories so big you could hide and not be found
Now tell me what harm ever came of depositories of books?

Procedural

The Old Fox sits at the front in the Chairman's eye, he
Questions the Apologies for Absence, he
Questions the Minutes, including
The accuracy of the amendments in these Minutes
To the Minutes of the meeting before last, he
Raises Matters Arising for half an hour.

Then he
Carps at the order of items on the Agenda,
Queries the omission of items *from* the Agenda,
Interrupts, interjects, raises Points of Information,
Asks innocent (loaded) questions, has serious Points of Order,
Puts down motions, puts down amendments to motions,
Puts down amendments to amendments, questions the voting,
Wants the Chairman to state exactly what it is
They have decided by the voting,
Wants his disagreement with the Chairman's decision minuted,
Quotes the Constitution,
Waves the Companies Act.

The Old Fox proposes the creation of
Sub-committees, steering committees, working parties and
Working Groups, and declines election
To any of them himself. Any Other Business
Is devoted to matters raised by the Old Fox alone.

When the time to decide the Date of Next Meeting arrives, he
Objects on sound grounds to every possible date.
The desk diaries wearily rise from dispatch cases once again,
The overcoats stay unbuttoned, the great white pages
Turn and flutter and the flutter becomes a wind
And the wind becomes a gale tearing
At the darkness outside the window,
At the darkness in everybody's soul in the steamed-up room.

When the storm subsides, the Old Fox
Has disappeared until the next time.

Notes

WARMTH and TEXAS BOOK DEPOSITORY. The method in both these poems might be described as a kind of satire by imitation. The naïve euphoria of the girl in 'Warmth' is captured in the repetition of fashionable jargon and calls into question the values of the media world on which she has become so emotionally dependent. In 'Texas Book Depository' the poem's entire structure is repetitive to the point of deliberate monotony, with the word 'depository' seeming to take on for the speaker such a significance that it is uttered with something approaching religious awe. The poem's satirical intent emerges from the discrepancy between the actual value of the book and the ironically insisted-on enthusiasm with which its establishment in the depository is celebrated. It was, incidentally, from the Texas School Book Depository in Dallas that Lee Harvey Oswald shot President Kennedy in 1963. This lends particular irony to the fact that the book in question is concerned with modern American history.

PROCEDURAL. This is one of several poems which describe the cunning strategies of the Old Fox. His skill is always to seem busy and public-spirited and yet to avoid taking any personal action or responsibility. He is an endearing master of guileful tactics, a mock hero, a survivor.

Peter Redgrove

Peter Redgrove was born in 1932. He studied science at Cambridge, and behind a good deal of his work there is the sense of a passionate scientist, someone who understands the physical laws of the universe but who at the same time sees them as a kind of magic. Redgrove has an imaginative richness which sometimes looks wildly eccentric, mystical and comic at the same time. He writes with intense conviction, copiously and often playfully. In his earlier work, he was seen to be something of the same sort of writer as Ted Hughes; but though both Hughes and Redgrove are possibly romantic soothsayers, and though their inspiration can often be seen as basically irrational, Redgrove is a much more careful organiser of language than is Hughes – at least in his most recent manifestations.

The Force

At Mrs Tyson's farmhouse, the electricity is pumped
Off her beck-borne wooden wheel outside.
Greased, steady, it spins within
A white torrent, that stretches up the rocks.
At night its force bounds down
And shakes the lighted rooms, shakes the light;
The mountain's force comes towering down to us.

High near its summit the brink is hitched
To an overflowing squally tarn.
It trembles with stored storms
That pulse across the rim to us, as light.

On a gusty day like this the force
Lashes its tail, the sky abounds
With wind-stuffed rinds of cloud that sprout
Clear force, throbbing in squalls off the sea
Where the sun stands poring down at itself
And makes the air grow tall in spurts
Whose crests turn over in the night-wind, foaming. We spin
Like a loose wheel, and throbbing shakes our light
Into winter, and torrents dangle. Sun
Pulls up the air in fountains, green shoots, forests
Flinching up at it in spray of branches,
Sends down clear water and the loosened torrent
Down into Mrs Tyson's farmhouse backyard,
That pumps white beams off its crest,
In a stiff breeze lashes its tail down the rocks.

Mr Waterman

'Now, we're quite private in here. You can tell me your troubles. The pond, I think you said . . .'

'We never really liked that pond in the garden. At times it was choked with a sort of weed, which, if you pulled one thread, gleefully unravelled until you had an empty basin before you and the whole of the pond in a soaking heap at your side. Then at other times it was as clear as gin, and lay in the grass staring upwards. If you came anywhere near, the gaze shifted sideways, and it was you that was being stared at, not the empty sky. If you were so bold as to come right up to the edge, swaggering and talking loudly to show you were not afraid, it presented you with so perfect a reflection that you stayed there spellbound and nearly missed dinner getting to know yourself. It had hypnotic powers.'

'Very well. Then what happened?'

'Near the pond was a small bell hung on a bracket, which the milkman used to ring as he went out to tell us upstairs in the bedroom that we could go down and make the early-morning

137

tea. This bell was near a little avenue of rose-trees. One morning, very early indeed, it tinged loudly and when I looked out I saw that the empty bottles we had put out the night before were full of bright green pondwater. I had to go down and empty them before the milkman arrived. This was only the beginning. One evening I was astounded to find a brace of starfish coupling on the ornamental stone step of the pool, and, looking up, my cry to my wife to come and look was stifled by the sight of a light peppering of barnacles on the stems of the rose-trees. The vermin had evidently crept there, taking advantage of the thin film of moisture on the ground after the recent very wet weather. I dipped a finger into the pond and tasted it: it was brackish.'

'But it got worse.'

'It got worse: one night of howling wind and tempestuous rain I heard muffled voices outside shouting in rural tones: "Belay there, you lubbers!" "Box the foresail capstan!" "A line! A line! Give me a line there, for Davy Jones' sake!" and a great creaking of timbers. In the morning, there was the garden-seat, which was too big to float, dragged tilting into the pond, half in and half out.'

'But you could put up with all this. How did the change come about?'

'It was getting playful, obviously, and inventive, if ill-informed, and might have got dangerous. I decided to treat it with the consideration and dignity which it would probably later have insisted on, and I invited it in as a lodger, bedding it up in the old bathroom. At first I thought I would have to run canvas troughs up the stairs so it could get to its room without soaking the carpet, and I removed the flap from the letter-box so it would be free to come and go, but it soon learnt to keep its form quite well, and get about in macintosh and goloshes, opening doors with gloved fingers.'

'Until a week ago . . .'

'A week ago it started sitting with us in the lounge (and the electric fire had to be turned off, as the windows kept on steaming up). It had accidentally included a goldfish in its body, and when the goggling dolt swam up the neck into the crystal-clear head, it dipped its hand in and fumbled about with many ripples and grimaces, plucked it out, and offered the fish to my wife, with a polite nod. She was just about to go into the kitchen and cook the supper, but I explained quickly that goldfish were bitter to eat, and he put it back. However, I was going to give him a big plate of ice-cubes, which he would have popped into his head and enjoyed sucking, although his real tipple is distilled water, while we watched television, but he didn't seem to want anything. I suppose he thinks he's big enough already.'

'Free board and lodging, eh?'

'I don't know what rent to charge him. I thought I might ask him to join the river for a spell and bring us back some of the money that abounds there: purses lost overboard from pleasure-steamers, rotting away in the mud, and so forth. But he has grown very intolerant of dirt, and might find it difficult to get clean again. Even worse, he might not be able to free himself from his rough dirty cousins, and come roaring back as an impossible green seething giant, tall as the river upended, buckling into the sky, and swamp us and the whole village as well. I shudder to think what would happen if he got as far as the sea, his spiritual home: the country would be in danger. I am at my wits' end, for he is idle, and lounges about all day.'

'Well, that's harmless enough . . .'

'If he's not lounging, he toys with his shape, restlessly. Stripping off his waterproof, he is a charming dolls'-house of glass, with doors and windows opening and shutting; a tree that thrusts up and fills the room; a terrifying shark-shape that darts about between the legs of the furniture, or lurks in the shadows of the room, gleaming in the light of the television-tube; a fountain that blooms without spilling a drop; or, and this image constantly recurs, a very small man with a very large head and streaming eyes, who gazes mournfully up at my wife (she takes no notice), and collapses suddenly into his tears with a sob and a gulp. Domestic, pastoral-phallic, maritime-ghastly, stately-gracious or grotesque-pathetic: he rings the changes on a gamut of moods, showing off, while I have to sit aside slumped in my armchair unable to compete, reflecting what feats he may be able to accomplish in due course with his body, what titillating shapes impose, what exaggerated parts deploy, under his macintosh. I dread the time (for it will come) when I shall arrive home unexpectedly early, and hear a sudden scuffle away in the wastepipes, and find my wife ("just out of the shower, dear") with that moist look in her eyes, drying her hair: and then to hear him swaggering in from the garden drains, talking loudly about his day's excursion, as if nothing at all had been going on. For he learns greater charm each day, this Mr Waterman, and can be as stubborn as winter and gentle as the warm rains of spring.'

'*I should say that you have a real problem there, but it's too early for a solution yet, until I know you better. Go away, take a week off from the office, spend your time with your wife, relax, eat plenty of nourishing meals, plenty of sex and sleep. Then come and see me again. Good afternoon.*'

'*The next patient, nurse. Ah, Mr Waterman. Sit down, please. Does the gas fire trouble you? No? I can turn it off if you wish. Well now, we're quite private in here. You can tell me your troubles. A married, air-breathing woman, I think you said . . .*'

The Idea of Entropy at Maenporth Beach

'*C'est elle! Noire et pourtant lumineuse.*'

A boggy wood as full of springs as trees.
Slowly she slipped into the muck.
It was a white dress, she said, and that was not right.
Leathery polished mud, that stank as it split.
It is a smooth white body, she said, and that is not right,
Not quite right; I'll have a smoother,
Slicker body, and my golden hair
Will sprinkle rich goodness everywhere.
So slowly she backed into the mud.
If it were a white dress, she said, with some little black,
Dressed with a little flaw, a smut, some swart
Twinge of ancestry, or if it were all black
Since I am white, but – it's my mistake.
So slowly she slunk, all pleated, into the muck.

The mud spatters with rich seed and ranging pollens.
Black darts up the pleats, black pleats
Lance along the white ones, and she stops
Swaying, cut in half. Is it right, she sobs
As the fat, juicy, incredibly tart muck rises
Round her throat and dims the diamond there?
It is right, so she stretches her white neck back
And takes a deep breath once and a one step back.
Some golden strands afloat pull after her.

The mud recoils, lies heavy, queasy, swart.
But then this soft blubber stirs, and quickly she comes up
Dressed like a mound of lickerish earth,
Swiftly ascending in a streaming pat
That grows tall, smooths brimming hips, and steps out
On flowing pillars, darkly draped.
And then the blackness breaks open with blue eyes
Of this black Venus rising helmeted in night
Who as she glides grins brilliantly, and drops
Swatches superb as molasses on her path.

Who is that negress running on the beach
Laughing excitedly with teeth as white
As the white waves kneeling, dazzled, to the sands?
Clapping excitedly the black rooks rise,
Running delightedly in slapping rags
She sprinkles substance, and the small life flies!

She laughs aloud, and bares her teeth again, and cries:
Now that I am all black, and running in my richness
And knowing it a little, I have learnt
It is quite wrong to be all white always;
And knowing it a little, I shall take great care
To keep a little black about me somewhere.
A snotty nostril, a mourning nail will do.
Mud is a good dress, but not the best.
Ah, watch, she runs into the sea. She walks
In streaky white on dazzling sands that stretch

Like the whole world's pursy mud quite purged.
The black rooks coo like doves, new suns beam
From every droplet of the shattering waves,
From every crystal of the shattered rock.
Drenched in the mud, pure white rejoiced,
From this collision were new colours born,
And in their slithering passage to the sea
The shrugged-up riches of deep darkness sang.

Notes

THE FORCE. Like so many of Redgrove's poems, this is a celebration of natural energy. Beginning and ending with the precise location of Mrs Tyson's farmhouse, it dazzles between these two points (one might almost call them terminals) with a descriptive power in which poetic imagination and scientific accuracy reinforce each other.

MR WATERMAN. An entertaining piece which is remarkably similar to the work of various absurdist playwrights, notably Eugene Ionesco and his English counterpart (popular in the early 1960s) N. F. Simpson. However, the 'twist' at the end raises a whole new set of questions and ensures that 'Mr Waterman' cannot be viewed simply as a whimsical exercise in surreal topsy-turvydom.

THE IDEA OF ENTROPY AT MAENPORTH BEACH. In her introduction to Redgrove's 'Sons of My Skin' (*Selected Poems 1954–1974*), a short essay which serves as a useful general introduction to the poet's work, Marie Peel writes of this poem that though it is not specifically written as such it nevertheless does amount to a direct answer to Wallace Stevens's 'The Idea of Order at Key West'. 'In this' she points out, referring to Stevens's poem, 'sea and sky are given order and meaning for the poet by the beauty of the girl's song. Peter Redgrove endorses the creative power of the artist acknowledged here, but he knows that waves and sky have meaning in themselves, have energy and evolutionary power . . . His white singer enters the disorderly mud, "From the collision were new colours born" and new power for the poet.' Although Redgrove's viscous, voluptuous vocabulary is very different from the sonorous romanticism and aesthetic poise of Wallace Stevens, it is interesting to compare the two poems, particularly in the cadence of their closing lines which are remarkably similar in tone. *Entropy* is a scientific term meaning 'dissipation of energy'. The reference to 'black Venus rising helmeted in night' (line 31) seems a conscious allusion to Botticelli's radiant painting 'The Birth of Venus' for the purpose of making a deliberately startling contrast. In fact, the element of shock is important throughout the poem, jerking the reader towards new perspectives from which the apparently grotesque can be viewed as full of energy and worthy of celebration. The quotation at the beginning is from Baudelaire's poem 'Un Phantôme'.

Geoffrey Hill

Geoffrey Hill was born in 1932. His four books of poems, the first (*For the Unfallen*) published in 1959, have been more highly praised – both in Britain and in the United States – than almost any other postwar work, particularly by his fellow poets, of almost all persuasions. Yet he is an isolated figure, difficult, dense, immediately convincing in his tightly packed eloquence yet needing much care and thought in subsequent readings. He has been called a visionary in the tradition of William Blake, 'a poet of the Sublime', but he is a much more learned and referential poet than Blake, with an acute sophistication which is quite different from the knowingness of some poets of the 1950s and 1960s. His most recent books are *Mercian Hymns* (1971) and *Tenebrae* (1978).

Merlin

I will consider the outnumbering dead:
For they are the husks of what was rich seed.
Now, should they come together to be fed,
They would outstrip the locusts' covering tide.

Arthur, Elaine, Mordred; they are all gone
Among the raftered galleries of bone.
By the long barrows of Logres they are made one,
And over their city stands the pinnacled corn.

In Piam Memoriam

I

Created purely from glass the saint stands,
Exposing his gifted quite empty hands
Like a conjurer about to begin,
A righteous man begging of righteous men.

II

In the sun lily-and-gold-coloured,
Filtering the cruder light, he has endured,
A feature for our regard; and will keep;
Of worldly purity the stained archetype.

III

The scummed pond twitches. The great holly-tree,
Emptied and shut, blows clear of wasting snow,
The common, puddled substance: beneath,
Like a revealed mineral, a new earth.

Ovid in the Third Reich

non peccat, quaecumque potest peccasse negare,
solaque famosam culpa professa facit.
(Amores, III, xiv)

I love my work and my children. God
Is distant, difficult. Things happen.
Too near the ancient troughs of blood
Innocence is no earthly weapon.

I have learned one thing: not to look down
So much upon the damned. They, in their sphere,
Harmonise strangely with the divine
Love. I, in mine, celebrate the love-choir.

Funeral Music

3

They bespoke doomsday and they meant it by
God, their curved metal rimming the low ridge.
But few appearances are like this. Once
Every five hundred years a comet's
Over-riding stillness might reveal men
In such array, livid and featureless,
With England crouched beastwise beneath it all.
'Oh, that old northern business . . .' A field
After battle utters its own sound
Which is like nothing on earth, but is earth.
Blindly the questing snail, vulnerable
Mole emerge, blindly we lie down, blindly
Among carnage the most delicate souls
Tup in their marriage-blood, gasping 'Jesus'.

6

My little son, when you could command marvels
Without mercy, outstare the wearisome
Dragon of sleep, I rejoiced above all –
A stranger well-received in your kingdom.
On those pristine fields I saw humankind
As it was named by the Father; fabulous
Beasts rearing in stillness to be blessed.
The world's real cries reached there, turbulence
From remote storms, rumour of solitudes,
A composed mystery. And so it ends.
Some parch for what they were; others are made
Blind to all but one vision, their necessity
To be reconciled. I believe in my
Abandonment, since it is what I have.

A Short History of British India (I)

Make miniatures of the once-monstrous theme:
the red-coat devotees, mêlées of wheels,
Jagannath's lovers. With indifferent aim
unleash the rutting cannon at the walls

of forts and palaces; pollute the wells.
Impound the memoirs for their bankrupt shame,
fantasies of true destiny that kills
'under the sanction of the English name'.

Be moved by faith, obedience without fault,
the flawless hubris of heroic guilt,
the grace of visitation; and be stirred

by all her god-quests, her idolatries,
in conclave of abiding injuries,
sated upon the stillness of the bride.

A Short History of British India (II)

Suppose they sweltered here three thousand years
patient for our destruction. There is a greeting
beyond the act. Destiny is the great thing,
true lord of annexation and arrears.

Our law-books overrule the emperors.
The mango is the bride-bed of light. Spring
jostles the flame-tree. But new mandates bring
new images of faith, good subahdars!

The flittering candles of the wayside shrines
melt into dawn. The sun surmounts the dust.
Krishna from Radha lovingly untwines.

147

Lugging the earth, the oxen bow their heads.
The alien conscience of our days is lost
among the ruins and on endless roads.

Mercian Hymns

I

King of the perennial holly-groves, the riven sandstone: over-
    lord of the M5: architect of the historic rampart and ditch,
    the citadel at Tamworth, the summer hermitage in Holy
    Cross: guardian of the Welsh Bridge and the Iron Bridge:
    contractor to the desirable new estates: saltmaster: money-
    changer: commissioner for oaths: martyrologist: the friend of
    Charlemagne.

'I liked that,' said Offa, 'sing it again.'

VII

Gasholders, russet among fields. Milldams, marlpools that lay
    unstirring. Eel-swarms. Coagulations of frogs: once, with
    branches and half-bricks, he battered a ditchful; then sidled
    away from the stillness and silence.

Ceolred was his friend and remained so, even after the day of the
    lost fighter: a biplane, already obsolete and irreplaceable, two
    inches of heavy snub silver. Ceolred let it spin through a hole
    in the classroom-floorboards, softly, into the rat-droppings
    and coins.

After school he lured Ceolred, who was sniggering with fright,
    down to the old quarries, and flayed him. Then, leaving
    Ceolred, he journeyed for hours, calm and alone, in his pri-
    vate derelict sandlorry named *Albion*.

Brooding on the eightieth letter of *Fors Clavigera*, I speak this in
  memory of my grandmother, whose childhood and prime
  womanhood were spent in the nailer's darg.

The nailshop stood back of the cottage, by the fold. It reeked
  stale mineral sweat. Sparks had furred its low roof. In dawn-
  light the troughed water floated a damson-bloom of dust –

not to be shaken by posthumous clamour. It is one thing to
  celebrate the 'quick forge', another to cradle a face hare-
  lipped by the searing wire.

Brooding on the eightieth letter of *Fors Clavigera*, I speak this in
  memory of my grandmother, whose childhood and prime
  womanhood were spent in the nailer's darg.

Notes

MERLIN. An early poem, drawing on the Arthurian story. Merlin was the magician at Arthur's court, and the poem may be considered a lyrical meditation or elegy by him. Elaine fell in love with Launcelot, and died for love of him. Mordred was a traitor who was killed by Arthur for trying to usurp his kingdom. Logres was that part of the island ruled over by King Logrin, or Locrine.

IN PIAM MEMORIAM. The title ('in holy memory') is an inscription found in churchyard or church. The three separated stanzas are themselves set out almost as if they were inscriptions, making different but related statements. In the first, a depiction of a saint in a stained-glass window shows him in the attitude of supplication, with his hands stretched out, empty (and yet what he offers is 'a gift'), as a conjuror showing that he is concealing nothing, and as a beggar asking for something. In the second, there is regard for the different qualities of endurance – lasting, and suffering – suggested by the figure illuminated in glass (and the words 'worldly' and 'stained' must be particularly carefully weighed). In the third, the poem moves out into the natural world, beyond man-made artefacts, to suggest another dimension to the problem posed by the image of the saint.

OVID IN THE THIRD REICH. The Latin lines that preface the poem as epigraph are taken from the *Amores* of Ovid. They mean: 'She does not sin who is able to deny her sin: it is only acknowledged dishonour that makes the fault.' The speaker of the poem is given in the title, a celebrated Roman poet who was first in, and then out of, favour at the court of the Emperor Augustus, here seeing himself in terms of a supposed existence in Nazi Germany. Each phrase and word in this poem has to be weighed very carefully: the ambiguities and evasions of attitude are reflected in the ambiguities of the language. It begins with what may look like flat, declarative, unarguable statements; the first two lines offer three such statements, and one is left to make one's own connections between them. The artist loves his work and his children, his immediate earthly preoccupations; God and his ways are both remote and difficult to understand; 'Things happen': that is what life consists of, things happening, over which one does not necessarily have control. One has a sense of the artist deliberately avoiding contamination from things he does not understand, or want to understand – away in his Ivory Tower, perhaps. But innocence 'is no earthly weapon', as in the cliché 'no earthly use', but also carrying with it the idea that it cannot either protect or attack (is neutral, in fact), and in any case cannot be used on earth, in our mortal life. Innocence is a state of perfection in heaven. 'The ancient troughs of blood' suggest pagan sacrifice to the gods, but also massacre – as in the 'final solution' the Nazis attempted to bring to the Jews. To be too close to them makes one powerless to alleviate their suffering; they are not 'distant', like God, but their very nearness (though the implication is that one has had no active part in the matter, and has done no harm) renders one impotent. How to reconcile these things, then? The second stanza picks this up: 'not to look down' on the damned (the sacrificed Jews, one takes it) implies literally not looking down on the circles of hell and not despising them; because it may be – the artist almost convinces himself – that their suffering is a part of God's 'distant, difficult' plan. So is the artist, in his separate 'sphere', his different *métier*, writing his poems. The whole poem, poised on its slightly jarring off-rhymes, is a brilliant and chilling raising of the question what an artist should do in a cruel, repressive society.

FUNERAL MUSIC: 3 and 6. These are two of a sequence consisting of eight fourteen-line poems (not strictly sonnets, because they do not rhyme). In a long note on 'Funeral Music', Hill has written that he was 'attempting a florid grim music broken by grunts and shrieks', 'a commination [a recital of divine threats against sinners, part of the Liturgy] and an alleluia for the period popularly but inexactly known as the Wars of the Roses'. The sequence is prefaced with the names of three noblemen executed during this period in the mid- and late fifteenth century, the Duke of Suffolk, the Earl of Worcester, and Earl Rivers. Behind it, too, writes Hill, there is 'a distant fury of battle. Without attempting factual detail, I had in mind the Battle of Towton, fought on Palm Sunday, 1461' – probably the bloodiest battle ever fought in England, in which 26,000 men are reckoned to have been killed.

One of the difficulties in 'Funeral Music' is to establish, at any single point, who the speaker is. In 3, there seem to be at least three, perhaps four, 'voices': at the beginning, a commentator looking back at the event; a dismissive modern comment ('Oh, that old northern business . . .'); someone involved in the battle ('blindly we lie down'); and the final gasped cry, 'Jesus'. As always in Hill, words and phrases need to be carefully weighed, as in 'like nothing on earth' – a cliché which is restored to proper meaning by being balanced against 'but is earth': the horror of the battlefield is both intensified and made literal.

The speaker of 6 seems to be one of the dying on the battlefield, perhaps addressing his own flesh, now 'damned' – if we pick up a hint from the conclusion of 5, which ends with a colon, not a full stop, and therefore seems to lead directly into 6. The 'abandonment' is like that of those in Hell, cut off from God's presence, remembering 'those pristine fields' of Creation from which they are now separated. One question here, and throughout 'Funeral Music', is whether suffering can be reconciled.

A SHORT HISTORY OF BRITISH INDIA (I AND II). These are two sonnets from a group of three with the same overall title, the group itself being part of a sequence of thirteen sonnets called 'An Apology for the Revival of Christian Architecture in England'. The sequence turns out to be an extended, wide-ranging and elegiac lament for what has been lost – what Coleridge (in an epigraph which Hill uses as preface) called 'the spiritual, Platonic old England'. But it quickly becomes apparent that 'An Apology . . .' is not a piece of pious antiquarianism; the ambiguities and brutalities of what has been lost are searched out with Hill's usual scrupulousness.

These two sonnets give some idea of the flavour of the whole. In them, Hill blends Hindu mythology, the not-to-be-sneered-at sense of divine duty of some British imperialists, the cruelty that existed before British settlement and the different cruelty that followed it (reaching its peak in the Indian Mutiny). 'Jagannath' has been absorbed into our 'juggernaut' – a term which has become a cliché but which here, as so often in Hill, is restored to its proper place, taking its colouring both from its original and from what has succeeded it.

MERCIAN HYMNS. *Mercian Hymns* is a sequence of thirty prose poems. They develop Geoffrey Hill's preoccupation with the patterns and continuities which inform what we call history. Throughout the sequence – which is full of wit and solemnity – the past is felt to be alive in the present, and the King, Offa of Mercia who ruled from A.D. 757–796 on whom the poems centre, becomes at different times the poet himself in his childhood or as an adult. This results in a continuously imaginative interplay between history and autobiography, between a shared and a personal inheritance.

In an interesting essay on Hill in *50 Modern British Poets* (Pan Books, 1979), Michael Schmidt comments on the form of the hymns: 'they follow an ostensibly prose form, but it is better to regard the 'paragraphs' as long lines instead, opening as they do with a line set to full type measure, followed by other lines evenly indented. The poem is rigorously phrased rather than cadenced: that is, the through rhythm is replaced by short rhythmic runs: the phrases are juxtaposed.' Schmidt also points out that in many of the poems the verse movement – those 'short rhythmic runs' – is that of the Old English Riddle, and it is interesting to consider Hill's debt to, and adaptation of, Anglo-Saxon methods.

I. 'The Naming of Offa'. At the start of the sequence Offa is identified as a ubiquitous and tutelary presence. This hymn demonstrates clearly Hill's method of historical and topographical juxtaposition. The phrase 'contractor to the desirable new estates' is typical of Hill's gift for fashioning nuggets of historical perspective, compact phrases which expand in the imagination as one explores the words and their associations. In this case, notice how the word 'estate' suggests at the same time both the traditional wealth and spaciousness of privilege and the modern housing estate. We are made aware of different 'layers' simultaneously so that we gain a genuine *perception* of history. The changes which have occurred in the words 'contractor' (building?) and 'desirable' (residences?) could also be studied. It is neither to imply that Hill is drily scholastic nor that he is teasingly difficult if one suggests that the ideal companion, while reading these hymns, would be the largest dictionary available. In a real sense, *Mercian Hymns* takes its readers on an adventure through the history of the English language.

VII 'The Kingdom of Offa'. Here the poet's own childhood memories are the controlling factor, but ancient memory presses against the recent and personal at every point. Notice the name of the friend, and the word 'flayed' (line 13). Most obvious, of course, is the name of the derelict sand lorry, *Albion*. Albion was the ancient name of Britain.

XXV 'Opus Anglicanum'. The elegiac tone is made almost incantatory by the way in which the hymn opens and closes with the same paragraph. There is a stark simplicity which matches the solemn, liturgical syntax. The contrast between the rich language and the hard life experienced by the grandmother is a moving one. *Fors Clavigera* is John Ruskin's collection of letters to the workmen of Great Britain, published between 1871 and 1884. These letters cover a wide range of topics but the underlying theme is a concern for the redress of poverty and human misery. The word 'darg' is one which Ruskin uses in the eightieth letter: it signifies 'a day's work, the task of a day' (OED). Geoffrey Hill's own note on the 'searing wire' (line 11) is as follows: 'I seem not to have been strictly accurate. Hand-made nails were forged from rods. Wire was used for the 'French Nails' made by machine. But: 'wire' = 'metal wrought into the form of a slender rod or thread' (OED). 'Quick forge' (line 10) is between inverted commas because it is a quotation from the Chorus which begins the last act of Shakespeare's *Henry V*. Hill writes: 'The phrase requires acknowledgement but the source has no bearing on the poem.' Shades of the drollery to be found in T. S. Eliot's notes on *The Waste Land*!

Sylvia Plath

Sylvia Plath was born in America in 1932, completed her education in this country at Cambridge where she met and married Ted Hughes, and died in London in 1963. Her suicide and the spate of memoirs which followed it have created a Plath legend, and few readers have been able to come to her poetry without in some way being contaminated by this. Unquestionably, she is an important poet who deserves to become dissociated as soon as possible from the 'industry' which has grown up around her. The chilly brilliance that characterises her early work becomes increasingly animated by anxiety, and her last poems – full of the most spectacular imagery – are an obsessive amalgam of desolation and black humour. Sylvia Plath could also write with an engaging, sprightly tenderness, particularly about her children, and it would be a mistake to see her as working at all times in a terrible isolation. Her *Collected Poems* were published in 1981 (Faber).

Mushrooms

Overnight, very
Whitely, discreetly,
Very quietly

Our toes, our noses
Take hold on the loam,
Acquire the air.

Nobody sees us,
Stops us, betrays us;
The small grains make room.

Soft fists insist on
Heaving the needles,
The leafy bedding,

Even the paving.
Our hammers, our rams,
Earless and eyeless,

Perfectly voiceless,
Widen the crannies,
Shoulder through holes. We

Diet on water,
On crumbs of shadow,
Bland-mannered, asking

Little or nothing.
So many of us!
So many of us!

We are shelves, we are
Tables, we are meek,
We are edible,

Nudgers and shovers
In spite of ourselves.
Our kind multiplies:

We shall by morning
Inherit the earth.
Our foot's in the door.

Spinster

Now this particular girl
During a ceremonious April walk
With her latest suitor
Found herself, of a sudden, intolerably struck
By the birds' irregular babel
And the leaves' litter.

By this tumult afflicted, she
Observed her lover's gestures unbalance the air,
His gait stray uneven
Through a rank wilderness of fern and flower.
She judged petals in disarray,
The whole season, sloven.

How she longed for winter then! —
Scrupulously austere in its order
Of white and black
Ice and rock, each sentiment within border,
And heart's frosty discipline
Exact as a snowflake.

But here — a burgeoning
Unruly enough to pitch her five queenly wits
Into vulgar motley —
A treason not to be borne. Let idiots
Reel giddy in bedlam spring:
She withdrew neatly.

And round her house she set
Such a barricade of barb and check
Against mutinous weather
As no mere insurgent man could hope to break
With curse, fist, threat
Or love, either.

Stillborn

These poems do not live: it's a sad diagnosis.
They grew their toes and fingers well enough,
Their little foreheads bulged with concentration.
If they missed out on walking about like people
It wasn't for any lack of mother-love.

O I cannot understand what happened to them!
They are proper in shape and number and every part.
They sit so nicely in the pickling fluid!
They smile and smile and smile and smile at me.
And still the lungs won't fill and the heart won't start.

They are not pigs, they are not even fish,
Though they have a piggy and a fishy air —
It would be better if they were alive, and that's what they were.
But they are dead, and their mother near dead with distraction,
And they stupidly stare, and do not speak of her.

Candles

They are the last romantics, these candles:
Upside down hearts of light tipping wax fingers,
And the fingers, taken in by their own haloes,
Grown milky, almost clear, like the bodies of saints.
It is touching, the way they'll ignore

A whole family of prominent objects
Simply to plumb the deeps of an eye
In its hollow of shadows, its fringe of reeds,
And the owner past thirty, no beauty at all.
Daylight would be more judicious,

Giving everybody a fair hearing.
They should have gone out with balloon flights and the
    stereopticon.
This is no time for the private point of view.
When I light them, my nostrils prickle.
Their pale, tentative yellows

Drag up false, Edwardian sentiments,
And I remember my maternal grandmother from Vienna.
As a schoolgirl she gave roses to Franz Josef.
The burghers sweated and wept. The children wore white.
And my grandfather moped in the Tyrol,

Imagining himself a headwaiter in America,
Floating in a high-church hush
Among ice buckets, frosty napkins.
These little globes of light are sweet as pears.
Kindly with invalids and mawkish women,

They mollify the bald moon.
Nun-souled, they burn heavenward and never marry.
The eyes of the child I nurse are scarcely open.
In twenty years I shall be retrograde
As these draughty ephemerids.

I watch their spilt tears cloud and dull to pearls.
How shall I tell anything at all
To this infant still in a birth-drowse?
Tonight, like a shawl, the mild light enfolds her,
The shadows stoop over like guests at a christening.

Among the Narcissi

Spry, wry, and grey as these March sticks,
Percy bows, in his blue peajacket, among the narcissi.
He is recuperating from something on the lung.

The narcissi, too, are bowing to some big thing:
It rattles their stars on the green hill where Percy
Nurses the hardship of his stitches, and walks and walks.

There is a dignity to this; there is a formality –
The flowers vivid as bandages, and the man mending.
They bow and stand: they suffer such attacks!

And the octogenarian loves the little flocks.
He is quite blue; the terrible wind tries his breathing.
The narcissi look up like children, quickly and whitely.

Lady Lazarus

I have done it again.
One year in every ten
I manage it –

A sort of walking miracle, my skin
Bright as a Nazi lampshade,
My right foot

A paperweight,
My face a featureless, fine
Jew linen.

Peel off the napkin
O my enemy.
Do I terrify? –

The nose, the eye pits, the full set of teeth?
The sour breath
Will vanish in a day.

Soon, soon the flesh
The grave cave ate will be
At home on me

And I a smiling woman.
I am only thirty.
And like the cat I have nine times to die.

This is Number Three.
What a trash
To annihilate each decade.

What a million filaments.
The peanut-crunching crowd
Shoves in to see

Them unwrap me hand and foot —
The big strip tease.
Gentlemen, ladies

These are my hands
My knees.
I may be skin and bone,

Nevertheless, I am the same, identical woman.
The first time it happened I was ten.
It was an accident.

The second time I meant
To last it out and not come back at all.
I rocked shut

As a seashell.
They had to call and call
And pick the worms off me like sticky pearls.

Dying
Is an art, like everything else.
I do it exceptionally well.

I do it so it feels like hell.
I do it so it feels real.
I guess you could say I've a call.

It's easy enough to do it in a cell.
It's easy enough to do it and stay put.
It's the theatrical

Comeback in broad day
To the same place, the same face, the same brute
Amused shout:

'A miracle!'
That knocks me out.
There is a charge

For the eyeing of my scars, there is a charge
For the hearing of my heart —
It really goes.

And there is a charge, a very large charge
For a word or a touch
Or a bit of blood

Or a piece of my hair or my clothes.
So, so, Herr Doktor.
So, Herr Enemy.

I am your opus,
I am your valuable,
The pure gold baby

That melts to a shriek.
I turn and burn.
Do not think I underestimate your great concern.

Ash, ash —
You poke and stir.
Flesh, bone, there is nothing there —

A cake of soap,
A wedding ring,
A gold filling.

Herr God, Herr Lucifer
Beware
Beware.

Out of the ash
I rise with my red hair
And I eat men like air.

You're

Clownlike, happiest on your hands,
Feet to the stars, and moon-skulled,
Gilled like a fish. A common-sense
Thumbs-down on the dodo's mode.
Wrapped up in yourself like a spool,
Trawling your dark as owls do.
Mute as a turnip from the Fourth
Of July to All Fools' Day,
O high-riser, my little loaf.

Vague as fog and looked for like mail.
Farther off than Australia.
Bent-backed Atlas, our travelled prawn.
Snug as a bud and at home
Like a sprat in a pickle jug.
A creel of eels, all ripples.
Jumpy as a Mexican bean.
Right, like a well-done sum.
A clean slate, with your own face on.

Notes

MUSHROOMS. Without its title, this poem would stand effectively as a riddle in the Anglo-Saxon vein. It gives a voice and character to these insidious 'nudgers and shovers' who announce themselves with increasing relentlessness. Their very blandness and meekness becomes a threat, and as the poem progresses, the precise natural observation (for example, stanza 4) is heightened by touches of almost Gothic horror. Lying, ironically, behind the last three stanzas are words from Christ's sermon on the mount: 'Blessed are the meek for they shall inherit the earth' (Matthew 5:5).

SPINSTER. This poem is particularly worth studying for the effect of its diction. The theme is a familiar one: the contrast between a temperament which needs to keep 'each sentiment within border' (stanza 3) and the vigour of spring. The spinster retreats (notice the siege imagery in the final stanza) into a winter of the spirit, denying her sexuality. The brittle phrasing and careful balancing of full and half rhymes seem most appropriate to the subject, and there is a fastidiousness of vocabulary in the lines describing the effects of spring (for example, 'Let idiots/ Reel giddy in bedlam spring') which underlines the spinster's recoil from all that is not 'scrupulously austere'.

STILLBORN. This poem describes an experience all too familiar to poets, the awareness that one has made something which looks exactly like a poem but which has gone dead between the mind and the page. The initial quickening has resulted in stillbirth. Sylvia Plath is able to communicate this experience with particular feeling by drawing on the intimate concern a mother has for her child at the moment of birth.

CANDLES. The candles become the central image in a meditation on light and shadow, youth and age, the present and the past. Franz Josef (1830–1916) was the Emperor of Austria-Hungary. The Tyrol is an Alpine province of Austria, lying between Bavaria and Italy. To be 'retrograde' (stanza 6) is to show a backward motion, to decline. The word is used in its astronomical sense, developing the image of the bald moon (stanza 6), the moon being a traditional emblem of woman. At the same time, of course, candles do literally decline as they burn away, thus symbolising the passing of life: compare Macbeth's 'Out, out, brief candle' on hearing of the death of his wife. A 'stereopticon' (stanza 3) is an early type of magic lantern designed to project a 'three-dimensional' picture. 'Ephemerids' (stanza 6) are small, shortlived insects.

AMONG THE NARCISSI. The phrase 'there is a formality' (stanza 3) suggests a way of looking at this poem. The old man and the flowers are seen as curiously and vividly united, both of them 'bowing to some big thing'. An interesting comparison can be made with Dylan Thomas's 'The force that through the green fuse drives the flower'. A peajacket (stanza 1) is a short overcoat of coarse woollen cloth worn by sailors.

LADY LAZARUS. The biblical account of Lazarus, who was brought back from the dead after four days in the grave, can be found in chapters 11 and 12 of St John's Gospel. It is part of the strength of this poem that Sylvia Plath never loses sight of the Lazarus story however obsessively she develops its application to her own suicidal urge, and a reading of the Bible account should increase admiration for her artistry. The speaker of the poem is fascinated by death which is personified as a doctor in a Nazi concentration camp, and much of the horror at the heart of the poem lies in the attitude she has towards him. She is the active victim who *needs* the persecutor in order to confirm her identity. The poem draws on the world of circus, striptease, American evangelism, Nazi brutality, and develops an alarming but clearly necessary sense of audience for her suffering. The constant changes of rhythm and pace reflect the speaker's state of excitement, as do some of the clusters of repeated rhyme sounds.

YOU'RE. A poem to be read and re-read by anyone who thinks of Sylvia Plath only as a poet of extremity and the dark. It is a generously imaginative address by a mother to her unborn child, full of invention and rhythmic variety. One effect which seems particularly happy comes in the line 'Right, like a well-done sum' where 'right' is isolated in such a way that, when read, it jumps suddenly (following the simile of the Mexican bean) enacting the unpredictable movement of the child in the womb.

Peter Scupham

Peter Scupham was born in 1933, but did not produce a collection until 1972 when his was the first volume in Harry Chambers's Peterloo Poets series, which has since become one of the liveliest poetry publishing ventures of the past few years. One of his reviewers has described Scupham's conspicuously elegant style as 'a stratagem, a way of writing affirmative poetry in a cynical age'. This rightly acknowledges what his detractors fail to recognise; they seize on the unfashionably decorative surfaces of his work and miss the moral passion and deep sense of historical continuity which inform them. Like Geoffrey Hill, Scupham can be uncompromising in his requirement of a certain degree of scholarship in his readers, but this is unlikely to deter the intelligent readership he seeks. His most recent collection is *Summer Palaces* (1980).

The Nondescript

I am plural. My intents are manifold:
I see through many eyes. I am fabulous.

I assimilate the suffering of monkeys:
Tiger and musk-ox are at my disposal.

My ritual is to swallow a pale meat
Prepared by my ignorant left hand.

It is my child's play to untie a frog,
Humble further the worm and dogfish.

When I comb the slow pond,
I shake out a scurf of tarnished silver;

When I steer the long ship to the stones,
A brown sickness laps at the cliff's foot.

Shreds of fur cling to my metalled roads,
Old plasters seeping a little blood.

I dress and powder the wide fields:
They undergo my purgatorial fires.

Come with me. I will shake the sky
And watch the ripe birds tumble.

It requires many deaths to ease
The deep cancer in my marrowbones.

I have prepared a stone inheritance.
It flourishes beneath my fertile tears.

Outing for the Handicapped Children

The held boat rocks to the staithe. Cautious, absorbed,
The children coax their limbs to their intent.
Her crutch blinks in the sun. Cheated by absent muscles,
He sinks with dazed acceptance to the grass.
About them, nervous in the gentle air,
Hands hover and fuss, glad to be ignored.

The day swells, unfolds. Laughter, scattered talk.
We hoist through dripping locks, part the dry sedges,
Plotting a fluent course by trees and swans
While summer, soft and potent, blurs through the awning,
Soaking the varnished wood. Torpid as grounded bees,
Their dangled fingers comb the river's skin.

They manage, patient, share with buns and fruit
A shaming kindness. Tamed, drowsy, separate,
We offer them our slow unnatural smiles;
Tremble with intimations of their pain.
The day we gave, or stole, edges away;
The cool depths pull their faces from the light.

Answers to Correspondents

Girls' Own, 1881

Queen of Trifles, we must consider your question
    Puerile and foolish in the last degree,
And May Bird, while we thank her for the letter,
    Must be less extravagant with the letter 't'.
Hester, imagine the sum required for investment
    If all could claim a pension who were born at sea.

Paquerelle, we fall back on the language of the Aesthetics:
    Your composition is quite too utterly too too;
Joanna, ask the cook. Gertrude, we are uncertain –
    What do you mean by 'will my writing do?'
Do what? Walk, talk or laugh? Maud, we believe and hope
    The liberties taken were not encouraged by you.

Constant Reader, if, as you hint, they are improper,
    We still do not see how to alter your cat's eyes;
Marinella, your efforts to remove tattoo-marks
    Are wasted. Wear longer sleeves. We do not advise
Cutting or burning. Smut, we could never think it
    A waste of time to make you better, and wise.

Tiny, the rage for old china is somewhat abated;
    Sunbeam, we are ignorant how you could impart
Bad habits to a goldfish. Inquisitive Mouse,
    Your spelling is a wretched example of the art.
Little Wych Hazel, we know no way but washing;
    Rusticus, may God's grace fill your heart.

Toujours Gai, your moulting canary needs a tonic;
   Xerxes, write poetry if you wish, but only read prose.
Cambridge Senior, we should not really have imagined
   It would require much penetration to disclose
That such answers as we supply have been elicited
   By genuine letters. You are impertinent, Rose.

Notes

THE NONDESCRIPT. Charles Waterton, the Victorian naturalist, created the Nondescript. It was the body of a Howler monkey on which he had, by his skill in taxidermy, modelled the features of a human face, and which he placed on the landing of his house in order to tease his visitors and gratify his own droll sense of humour. This poem is concerned with the abuse, by man, of the natural world. It was first published in *The Observer* with the subtitle 'A Poem for Conservation Year', and it makes several references to contemporary events and practice although its impact is made without the need for precise identification. A few notes might be helpful, though. Stanza 2 makes reference to the use of animal secretions for medicinal and cosmetic purposes. The 'pale meat' of stanza 3 is veal, and the 'ignorant left hand' has behind it both the full weight of the Latin sinister (left) and the biblical reference to the right hand not knowing what the left does. The 'brown sickness' refers to the pollution of the Cornish shores by oil and smoke when the tanker Torrey Canyon was wrecked, and subsequently dive-bombed by RAF planes in an unsuccessful attempt to burn off the oil (1967). The poem's construction, in closed unrhyming couplets, contributes to its forceful effect. The tone is uncompromisingly blunt, but the language is memorably metaphorical.

171

OUTING FOR THE HANDICAPPED CHILDREN. With an attention to small illuminating detail which is characteristic of Peter Scupham's work, a mood of great tenderness and concern is created. The idyllic setting is juxtaposed with the children's pain and an awareness that what for others might be the pleasurable languor of relaxation is, for the children, the torpor of 'dazed acceptance' (stanza 1). Note that the adults' drowsiness – shared superficially with the children on this summer day – is of a totally 'separate' order (stanza 3). Scupham movingly defines the gap between the handicapped children and the healthy adults which can only be bridged by acts of kindness and 'slow unnatural smiles'.

ANSWERS TO CORRESPONDENTS. This is a kind of antique agony column and consists, with very little alteration, of actual answers given to those Victorian girls who wrote to *Girls' Own* in 1881. It is a light-hearted but revealing indication of the concerns and manners of well-bred young girls of the period. Are they any more trivial than many of the queries which can be read in the columns of present-day teenage magazines?

Seamus Heaney

Seamus Heaney was born in 1939 in Northern Ireland. His first collection, *Death of a Naturalist* (1966), drew largely on his rural childhood and was striking for the sensuous immediacy of its language. This gift for realising his themes in a poetry of considerable verbal strength and flexibility has enabled him to render some of the historical complexities behind the political strife in Northern Ireland without betraying his art. Adapting and dignifying the phrase 'internal émigré', used to brand the Russian poets Mandelstam and Akhmatova, Heaney has described himself as 'neither internee nor informer;/ An inner émigré, grown long-haired/ And thoughtful' ('Exposure'). Many of his finest recent poems seem to gather round the phrase, from the last stanza of 'The Harvest Bow' (see page 180), 'The end of art is peace', and can be seen as ritual enactments of harmony and reconciliation on deeply troubled ground.

Blackberry-Picking

For Philip Hobsbaum

Late August, given heavy rain and sun
For a full week, the blackberries would ripen.
At first, just one, a glossy purple clot
Among others, red, green, hard as a knot.
You ate that first one and its flesh was sweet
Like thickened wine: summer's blood was in it
Leaving stains upon the tongue and lust for
Picking. Then red ones inked up and that hunger
Sent us out with milk-cans, pea-tins, jam-pots
Where briars scratched and wet grass bleached our boots.
Round hayfields, cornfields and potato-drills
We trekked and picked until the cans were full,
Until the tinkling bottom had been covered
With green ones, and on top big dark blobs burned
Like a plate of eyes. Our hands were peppered
With thorn pricks, our palms sticky as Bluebeard's.

We hoarded the fresh berries in the byre.
But when the bath was filled we found a fur,
A rat-grey fungus, glutting on our cache.
The juice was stinking too. Once off the bush
The fruit fermented, the sweet flesh would turn sour.
I always felt like crying. It wasn't fair
That all the lovely canfuls smelt of rot.
Each year I hoped they'd keep, knew they would not.

Undine

He slashed the briars, shovelled up grey silt
To give me right of way in my own drains
And I ran quick for him, cleaned out my rust.

He halted, saw me finally disrobed,
Running clear, with apparent unconcern.
Then he walked by me. I rippled and I churned

Where ditches intersected near the river
Until he dug a spade deep in my flank
And took me to him. I swallowed his trench

Gratefully, dispersing myself for love
Down in his roots, climbing his brassy grain –
But once he knew my welcome, I alone

Could give him subtle increase and reflection.
He explored me so completely, each limb
Lost its cold freedom. Human, warmed to him.

The Toome Road

One morning early I met armoured cars
In convoy, warbling along on powerful tyres,
All camouflaged with broken alder branches,
And headphoned soldiers standing up in turrets.
How long were they approaching down my roads
As if they owned them? The whole country was sleeping.
I had rights-of-way, fields, cattle in my keeping,
Tractors hitched to buckrakes in open sheds,
Silos, chill gates, wet slates, the greens and reds
Of outhouse roofs. Whom should I run to tell
Among all of those with their back doors on the latch
For the bringer of bad news, that small-hours visitant
Who, by being expected, might be kept distant?
Sowers of seed, erectors of headstones . . .
O charioteers, above your dormant guns,
It stands here still, stands vibrant as you pass,
The invisible, untoppled omphalos.

Freedman

*Indeed, slavery comes nearest to its justification in the early Roman Empire:
for a man from a 'backward' race might be brought within the pale of
civilization, educated and trained in a craft or a profession, and turned
into a useful member of society.*

R. H. Barrow: *The Romans*

Subjugated yearly under arches,
Manumitted by parchments and degrees,
My murex was the purple dye of lents
On calendars all fast and abstinence.

'*Memento homo quia pulvis es.*'
I would kneel to be impressed by ashes,
A silk friction, a light stipple of dust –
I was under that thumb too like all my caste.

One of the earth-starred denizens, indelibly,
I sought the mark in vain on the groomed optimi:
Their estimating, census-taking eyes
Fastened on my mouldy brow like lampreys.

Then poetry arrived in that city –
I would abjure all cant and self-pity –
And poetry wiped my brow and sped me.
Now they will say I bite the hand that fed me.

Punishment

I can feel the tug
of the halter at the nape
of her neck, the wind
on her naked front.

It blows her nipples
to amber beads,
it shakes the frail rigging
of her ribs.

I can see her drowned
body in the bog,
the weighing stone,
the floating rods and boughs.

Under which at first
she was a barked sapling
that is dug up
oak-bone, brain-firkin:

her shaved head
like a stubble of black corn,
her blindfold a soiled bandage,
her noose a ring

to store
the memories of love.
Little adulteress,
before they punished you

you were flaxen-haired,
undernourished, and your
tar-black face was beautiful.
My poor scapegoat,

I almost love you
but would have cast, I know,
the stones of silence.
I am the artful voyeur

of your brain's exposed
and darkened combs,
your muscles' webbing
and all your numbered bones:

I who have stood dumb
when your betraying sisters,
cauled in tar,
wept by the railings,

who would connive
in civilised outrage
yet understand the exact
and tribal, intimate revenge.

Orange Drums, Tyrone, 1966

The lambeg balloons at his belly, weighs
Him back on his haunches, lodging thunder
Grossly there between his chin and his knees.
He is raised up by what he buckles under.

Each arm extended by a seasoned rod,
He parades behind it. And though the drummers
Are granted passage through the nodding crowd
It is the drums preside, like giant tumours.

To every cocked ear, expert in its greed,
His battered signature subscribes 'No Pope'.
The pigskin's scourged until his knuckles bleed.
The air is pounding like a stethoscope.

The Seed Cutters

They seem hundreds of years away. Breughel,
You'll know them if I can get them true.
They kneel under the hedge in a half-circle
Behind a windbreak wind is breaking through.
They are the seed cutters. The tuck and frill
Of leaf-sprout is on the seed potatoes
Buried under that straw. With time to kill
They are taking their time. Each sharp knife goes
Lazily halving each root that falls apart
In the palm of the hand: a milky gleam,
And, at the centre, a dark watermark.
O calendar customs! Under the broom
Yellowing over them, compose the frieze
With all of us there, our anonymities.

The Harvest Bow

As you plaited the harvest bow
You implicated the mellowed silence in you
In wheat that does not rust
But brightens as it tightens twist by twist
Into a knowable corona,
A throwaway love-knot of straw.

Hands that aged round ashplants and cane sticks
And lapped the spurs on a lifetime of game cocks
Harked to their gift and worked with fine intent
Until your fingers moved somnambulant:
I tell and finger it like braille,
Gleaning the unsaid off the palpable,

And if I spy into its golden loops
I see us walk between the railway slopes
Into an evening of long grass and midges,
Blue smoke straight up, old beds and ploughs in hedges,
An auction notice on an outhouse wall –
You with a harvest bow in your lapel,

Me with the fishing rod, already homesick
For the big lift of these evenings, as your stick
Whacking the tips off weeds and bushes
Beats out of time, and beats, but flushes
Nothing: that original townland
Still tongue-tied in the straw tied by your hand.

The end of art is peace
Could be the motto of this frail device
That I have pinned up on our deal dresser –
Like a drawn snare
Slipped lately by the spirit of the corn
Yet burnished by its passage, and still warm.

Notes

BLACKBERRY-PICKING. Bluebeard (to be found in the French tale by Perrault) was a wealthy man of evil reputation who married several wives and killed all but the last one, Fatima, who discovered the bodies of her predecessors by entering a forbidden room, and managed to escape their fate in the nick of time. Given the poem's variation on the theme of innocence and experience, the reference (line 16) is curiously appropriate as well as being effectively bizarre. Not only does it provide a fittingly theatrical climax to a sequence of images which compare the blackberry juice with blood, but it also lays emphasis on the important stages of expectation, discovery and disenchantment on which the whole poem is based. A 'cache' is a hiding place for treasure. This is a subtly chosen word which matches the children's secret delight and contrasts dramatically with the sickening 'rat-grey fungus'. Notice that the half-rhyming couplets make way, on two occasions, for a full rhyme. The effect of this might be considered.

UNDINE. Undine was a female water sprite who, by marrying a mortal and bearing a child, might receive a soul. In this poem the myth becomes a metaphor for the process and rewards of good husbandry. Because the farmer respects the natural course of the water (stanza 1) he experiences its gratitude. In terms of the myth, the bearing of the child is implicit in the reference to the roots and grain (stanza 4) which will become the harvest, and in the last two lines of the poem a beautifully described Pygmalion-like transformation completes the story, suggesting the awakening of a human soul.

THE TOOME ROAD. The rhetorical first line of this poem is in the tradition of 'visionary encounters': 'One morning early, I met . . .' and the mystery is sustained as the poem develops, fusing a contemporary military operation with images drawn from early mythology. It is as if, ironically, the armoured cars were re-enacting a primitive ritual and the headphoned soldiers were priests placating strange gods. Ancient Ireland and present troubles are instantly identified in a disturbingly lyrical image (note, particularly, 'warbling' in line 2). 'The omphalos' is the conical stone at Delphi supposed to be the central point of the earth. Here it seems to stand for the centre, the hub.

FREEDMAN. The epigraph from a book about the Romans is there to throw an ironical historical light on the poem. Heaney is equating the historian's remarks about the relationship between Romans and 'backward' races with the relationship between Protestants and Catholics in Northern Ireland. A further ironical effect is given by the markedly Latinate diction of the poem – 'subjugated', 'manumitted', 'abstinence', and so on.

Roman captives were 'subjugated' – that is, forced to bow beneath a yoke: the Roman Catholic church subjugated the poet ('under arches'), but he was freed ('manumitted') by his education. Instead of the imperial purple of the rulers, his life was regulated by the obligations of fast days, indicated in purple on church calendars. At the Ash Wednesday services in Lent, he knelt to receive the priest's symbolic thumb-print of ash, creating a caste-mark (while the priest murmurs the Latin words – 'Remember man that thou art dust'). The Protestants, the favoured people ('optimi', stanza 3), wore no such mark: they recognised him as an inferior by it. Being educated and becoming a poet, he was set free from such discriminations – but now he will be accused of ingratitude.

PUNISHMENT. This is one of a number of Heaney's poems which take their imagery from the Iron Age corpses found preserved in the peat bogs of Denmark: his source was chiefly a book by the Danish archaeologist, P. V. Glob, *The Bog People*. The execution of the prehistoric girl is seen as analogous to the ritualistic punishment of women (presumed traitors) in Northern Ireland, who have been shaved and tarred by extremists as an 'example' to others. The poet is torn between 'conniving' and 'understanding' (stanza 11).

ORANGE DRUMS, TYRONE, 1966. A Protestant drummer in an Orange Day parade (celebrating the defeat of James II by William of Orange at the Battle of the Boyne in 1690). The 'lambeg' is a large ceremonial drum. In the poem, the exultant fanaticism and excitement of the man merges with the instrument, creating fear and foreboding.

182

THE SEED CUTTERS. The figures of the seed cutters, taking out the new growth from the potatoes for next year's crop, are seen as in a painting, such as those by the sixteenth century Flemish painter, Breughel, who portrayed many scenes of peasant life. What the seed cutters are doing is ancient: it forms a link with the past of Ireland, so much affected by the potato cycle. The harshness of weather, the almost ritualistic action of the seed cutters, and the continuity of both: these come together and are celebrated.

THE HARVEST BOW. This beautiful poem is, simultaneously, a poem about making and reconciliation. Notice how the poet's tenderly recalled relationship with the man who plaited harvest bows in his boyhood, the bow itself, and the inevitable political undertones in the statement *'The end of art is peace'* seem to unite past, present and future in an extended emblematic metaphor of great resonance and generosity.

Douglas Dunn

Douglas Dunn was born in 1942. Since his book *Terry Street* (1969) established him as a poet of serious social concern and original descriptive gifts, his work has developed and he has begun to handle large themes with impressive force. What makes him particularly interesting is the tension between those moral and political imperatives towards which he selfconsciously points his readers and the elegantly phrased, nostalgic yearnings which are constantly softening his rougher edges.

A Removal from Terry Street

On a squeaking cart, they push the usual stuff,
A mattress, bed ends, cups, carpets, chairs,
Four paperback westerns. Two whistling youths
In surplus U.S. Army battle-jackets
Remove their sister's goods. Her husband
Follows, carrying on his shoulders the son
Whose mischief we are glad to see removed,
And pushing, of all things, a lawnmower.
There is no grass in Terry Street. The worms
Come up cracks in concrete yards in moonlight.
That man, I wish him well. I wish him grass.

In the Grounds

Yorkshire, 1975

Barbarians in a garden, softness does
Approve of who we are as it does those
Who when we speak proclaim us barbarous
And say we have no business with the rose.

Gently the grass waves, and its green applauds
The justice, not of progress, but of growth.
We walk as people on the paths of gods
And in our minds we harmonize them both.

Disclosures of these grounds – a river view,
Two Irish wolfhounds watching on a lawn;
A spinster with her sewing stares at you,
And begs you leave her pretty world alone.

More books than prejudice in our young minds . . .
We could not harm her, would not, would prefer
A noise less military and more kind
Than our boots make across her wide *parterre*.

We are intransigent, at odds with them.
They see our rabble-dreams as new contempt
For England's art of house and leaf. Condemn
Our clumsiness – you do not know, how, unkempt

And coarse, we hurt a truth with truth, still true
To who we are: barbarians, whose chins
Drool with ale-stinking hair, whose horses chew
Turf owned by watching, frightened mandarins,

Their surly nephews lounging at each gate,
Afraid we'll steal their family's treasured things,
Then hawk them – pictures, furniture and plate –
Round the encampments of our saddle-kings.

Stories

Once, once, O once upon a time –
I wish that's how a poem could begin,
And so begin one. That's how stories should.
The sweet parental voices started so,
Opening a book, *my* book, one given by
An aunt and uncle, inscribed 'for Christmas'.

No story ever did, I think, unless
Its author, sitting down, said, 'O I wish
That *this* is how a story could begin',
And so began, his tongue half in his cheek.
Once, once, O once upon a time –
It's real, magnanimous, and true! I wish,

And wish, and so my friends lose patience with
My stories and they say, 'So this piece is
A story of lost gloves, and, yes, I know
I lost *my* gloves, but why this story, *this*,
This *making-up?'* Once, once, O once upon
A time, before gloves, gauntlets, politics . . .

Never, never, never, never, never . . .
That's a *good* line. And there was one which took
My senses to adventure on a day
Of wind and rain . . . 'One more step, Mr Hands,
And I'll blow your brains out!' *Once, once, once, once* . . .
I think the alphabet is tired of life.

'But be contemporary!' they shout, thumping
The table, and 'Yes, Yes', I say, 'I'll buy
That, all or nothing. Just you wait, you'll see.
I'm of the times . . . My pulse is topical,
And I love all the things I'm meant to love,
Am civil and 'sincere', one of the boys.'

Ah, that's better. I mean, I mean it *all*.
Yet when I start to write, my pen puts down
Once, once, O once upon a time . . .
And that's for nothing and for no one,
Not anyone, not even for a child
Who, at a table by a bowl of fruit,

Sits down to read. It is too personal,
One sorry pass. I'll give away my thought
Of knowing that a life-discarded petal
Fell down, so slowly, when, a child, I read,
And landed on a page and was brushed off.
Once, once, O once, that happened so, like that –

Tender descent – and for a moment was
Completed by its image on the polished
Table. I took it in, did not forget.
Then, *am* I good? Was *that* benevolent?
Now, dignity of tables and of books,
What do *you* say? *'There is no answer, friend.'*

Notes

A REMOVAL FROM TERRY STREET. Part of a group of poems written in and about a poor part of Hull. Dunn has said of his early 'Terry Street' poems that he 'tried to understand the familiar and the ordinary' and that it was never his intention 'that the poems be read as social or any other kind of protest'.

IN THE GROUNDS. To the Greeks, a barbarian was someone who did not speak their language. '*Bar-bar, bar-bar*' was the contemptuous noise they made to indicate these alien tongues. This poem's speaker is, it seems, one of a group of self-conscious, educated young men from the working class who feel themselves to be labelled and dismissed by an upper-class world which – they imagine – fears them to be envious and bent on harming the garden (and all that it stands for). A '*parterre*' (stanza 4) is a level space in a garden, occupied by flowerbeds. A 'mandarin' (stanza 6), despite its precise Chinese origin, here indicates a remote and fastidious aesthete. Notice the formality of the poem's rhyme scheme and metre. Is this intentionally ironic, given the speaker's view of himself as a barbarian?

STORIES. It is probably over simple to consider this poem as indicating the dilemma of a gifted, imaginative writer troubled by a social conscience which leads him to mistrust his own more private longings, but the argument it sets forth is certainly unresolved. In stanza 4 the first line is taken from the final scene of Shakespeare's *King Lear*, and Mr Hands is a character from R. L. Stevenson's *Treasure Island*. The tone of the poem's close shows how much Dunn has learnt from the later work of a fine American poet, Randall Jarrell.

Craig Raine

Craig Raine was born in 1944, educated at Oxford, where he later taught English at various colleges for a number of years, and is now poetry editor of Faber. His first book, *The Onion, Memory* (1977), was widely noticed and praised as showing a fantastic figurative invention, a kind of sprightly metaphorical astonishment at ordinary things extraordinarily observed. This continued in *A Martian Sends a Postcard Home* (1979), but perhaps with a slightly wider range. What limits Raine, and in our view prevents him being quite the bright hope of the future he has been claimed to be, is that the ingenuity becomes too much like a repeated party trick. At his best, though, there is a genuinely fresh eye at work, and considerable phrase-making skill.

A Martian Sends a Postcard Home

Caxtons are mechanical birds with many wings
and some are treasured for their markings –

they cause the eyes to melt
or the body to shriek without pain.

I have never seen one fly, but
sometimes they perch on the hand.

Mist is when the sky is tired of flight
and rests its soft machine on ground:

then the world is dim and bookish
like engravings under tissue paper.

189

Rain is when the earth is television.
It has the property of making colours darker.

Model T is a room with the lock inside –
a key is turned to free the world

for movement, so quick there is a film
to watch for anything missed.

But time is tied to the wrist
or kept in a box, ticking with impatience.

In homes, a haunted apparatus sleeps,
that snores when you pick it up.

If the ghost cries, they carry it
to their lips and soothe it to sleep

with sounds. And yet, they wake it up
deliberately, by tickling with a finger.

Only the young are allowed to suffer
openly. Adults go to a punishment room

with water but nothing to eat.
They lock the door and suffer the noises

alone. No one is exempt
and everyone's pain has a different smell.

At night, when all the colours die,
they hide in pairs

and read about themselves –
in colour, with their eyelids shut.

Flying to Belfast, 1977

It was possible to laugh
as the engines whistled to the boil,

and wonder what the clouds liked like –
shovelled snow, Apple Charlotte,

Tufty Tails . . . I enjoyed
the Irish Sea, the ships were faults

in a dark expanse of linen.
And then Belfast below, a radio

with its back ripped off,
among the agricultural abstract

of the fields. Intricate,
neat and orderly. The windows

gleamed like drops of solder –
everything was wired up.

I thought of wedding presents,
white tea things

grouped on a dresser,
as we entered the cloud

and were nowhere –
a bride in a veil, laughing

at the sense of event, only
half afraid of an empty house

with its curtains boiling
from the bedroom window.

Notes

A MARTIAN SENDS A POSTCARD HOME. The imagined innocent from another planet looks at life on our earth and tries to make sense of it in all its confusing detail: books, cars, watches and clocks, babies, lavatories, sleep and dreams. Identifying the individual images, relating them to what they 'really' are, is like solving a puzzle.

FLYING TO BELFAST, 1977. As in 'A Martian Sends a Postcard Home', but here the viewer is clearly a human being, the objects looked at are wrenched out of their ordinary contexts and seen in quite other terms. The similes and metaphors are homely and domesticated as well as fantastic; but flying to such a place at such a time carries with it an undercurrent of nervous laughter, which in the final image expands out into something much more like plain fear.

Acknowledgements

We are grateful to the following for permission to reproduce copyright material:

the author's agent for Charles Causley's poems 'My Friend Maloney', 'By St Thomas Water', 'Reservoir Street' and 'Conducting a Children's Choir' from *Collected Poems* published by Macmillan; Andre Deutsch for Roy Fuller's poems 'Translation', 'The Ides of March', 'Autobiography of a Lungworm' from *Collected Poems* and 'Homage to Balthus' from *Tiny Tears* and Geoffrey Hill's poems 'Merlin' from *For the Unfallen*, 'In Piam Memoriam', 'Ovid in the Third Reich', 'Funeral Music 3', 'Funeral Music 6' from *King Log*, 'A Short History of British India I and II' from *Tenebrae* and 'Mercian Hymns I, VII, XXV' from *Mercian Hymns*; the author's agent for Robert Graves' poems 'Here Live Your Life Out', 'Surgical Ward: Men', 'A Dream of Frances Speedwell', 'A Time of Waiting' and 'Dance of Words'); Hutchinson Publishing Group for Patricia Beer's poems 'After Death', 'Prochorus Thompson' and 'Arms' from *Selected Poems*; Macmillan, London and Basingstoke for R. S. Thomas' poems 'The Bright Field', 'The Moon in Lleyn', 'The Chapel' from *Laboratories of the Spirit*, 'Gone', 'Album' and 'Groping' from *Frequencies*; Eric Morten Publishers and the author, Peter Scupham for his poem 'The Nondescript'; John Murray Ltd for John Betjeman's poems 'NW5 and NW6', 'Executive' from *Collected Poems* and an extract from *Summoned by Bells*; Oxford University Press for Peter Scupham's poems 'Outing for the Handicapped Children' from *Prehistories* © Oxford University Press 1975, 'Answer to Correspondents: Girl's Own 1881' from *The Hinterland* © Oxford University Press 1977 and Craig Raine's poems 'A Martian Sends a Postcard Home' and 'Flying to Belfast 1977' from *A Martian Sends a Postcard Home* © Craig Raine 1979; the author's agent for Sylvia Plath's poems 'Mushrooms', 'Spinster' from *The Colossus* published by Faber and Faber © Ted Hughes 1967, 'Stillborn', 'Candles' 'Among the Narcissi' from *Crossing the Water* published by Faber and Faber © Ted Hughes 1971, 'Lady Lazarus' and 'You're' from *Ariel* published by Faber and Faber © Ted Hughes 1965; the author, Peter Porter and Oxford University Press for his poems 'A Consumer's Report' from *The Last of England* © Oxford University Press 1970, 'Mort aux Chats', 'May 1945' from *Preaching to the Converted* © Oxford University Press 1972 and 'An Angel in Blythburgh Church' from *The Cost of Seriousness* © Peter Porter 1978; Routledge and Kegan Paul Ltd for Peter Redgrove's poems 'The Force', 'Mr Waterman' and 'The Idea of Entropy at Maenporth Beach' from *Sons of My Skin*; the author, Vernon Scannell for his poems 'Dead Dog', 'Walking Wounded' and 'A Case of Murder'; the author, Alan Brownjohn and Martin Secker and Warburg Ltd for his poems 'Warmth', 'Texas Book Depository' from *A Song of Good Life* and

'Procedural' from *A Night In the Gazebo*; James MacGibbon, executor of Stevie Smith Estate for the poems 'Mrs Arbuthnot', 'The Donkey', 'Black March', 'Tenuous and Precarious' and 'Not Waving But Drowning' from *The Collected Poems of Stevie Smith*; Faber and Faber Ltd for the poems 'The Cave of Making', 'The Fall of Rome', 'The Shield of Achilles', 'August 1968', 'In Due Season' and 'Talking to Myself' from *Collected poems* by W. H. Auden; 'Apple Blossom', 'The Slow Starter', 'Old Masters Abroad', 'Soap Suds', 'The Truisms' and 'Thalassa' from *Collected poems* by Louis MacNeice; 'Love Songs in Age', 'Ambulances', 'The Whitsun Weddings' and 'An Arundel Tomb' from *The Whitsun Weddings* by Philip Larkin, 'The Old Fools', 'The Building', 'The Explosion' and 'The Trees' from *High Windows* by Philip Larkin; 'A Removal from Terry Street' from *Terry Street* by Douglas Dunn, 'In the Grounds' and 'Stories' from *Barbarians* by Douglas Dunn; 'On the Move' from *The Sense of Movement* by Thom Gunn, 'Innocence' from *My Sad Captains* by Thom Gunn, 'The Fair in the Woods' and 'The Discovery of the Pacific' from *Moly* by Thom Gunn, 'Back to Life' from *Touch* by Thom Gunn, 'Last Days at Teddington' from *Jack Straws Castle* by Thom Gunn; 'Hawk Roosting' from *The Hawk in the Rain* by Ted Hughes, 'Thistles' and 'Full Moon and Little Frieda' from *Wodwo* by Ted Hughes, 'Crow Goes Hunting' and 'A Childish Prank' from *Crow* by Ted Hughes, 'His Legs Ran About' from *Cave Birds* by Ted Hughes, 'The Stag' from *Season Songs* by Ted Hughes, 'Coming Down Through Somerset' from *Moortown* by Ted Hughes; 'Blackberry Picking' from *Death of a Naturalist* by Seamus Heaney, 'Undine' from *Door Into The Dark* by Seamus Heaney, 'The Toome Road' and 'The Harvest Bow' from *Fieldwork* by Seamus Heaney, 'Freedman', 'Punishment', 'Orange Drums, Tyrone, 1966', 'The Seed Cutters' from *North* by Seamus Heaney and The Marvell Press, England for 'Church Going' from *The Less Deceived* by Philip Larkin.

Charged with sedition, he was convicted and sentenced, but won on appeal to the House of Lords. Despairing of the continuing famine and negative prospects for Irish independence, he emigrated to Australia and became Premier of Victoria in 1871.

He was knighted in 1873, retired from politics and lived in France. He died in Nice in 1903, aged 86.

Sir William Macaulay, is based on Sir Randolph Routh, born in Poole, Dorset, in 1782.

He did military service in Jamaica, the Netherlands in the Welcheren Campaign, the Peninsular War, the Battle of Waterloo. He was promoted to Commissariat General of the British Army in 1826. He spent seventeen years as Colonial Administrator in Canada and was knighted in 1843. In 1845 Prime Minster Peel appointed him Chairman of the Irish Relief Commission. He was frequently at odds with Sir Charles Trevelyan.

Routh died in 1858, aged 76.

ABOUT THE AUTHOR

Michael Nicholson is one of the world's most travelled and decorated foreign correspondents. In a forty-year career in television
he has reported from eighteen war zones and was three times
Royal Television Society's Journalist of the Year. He was twice
'Emmy' finalist at the International Academy of Television Arts
and Sciences for documentaries and received a BAFTA award
for his reports from the Falklands War. He was also awarded the
Falklands and Gulf Campaign Medals and an OBE by Queen
Elizabeth II in 1991 for services to television.

In 1992 he smuggled Natasha, an orphan child, out of Bosnia.
Natasha's Story (Macmillan, 1993) was made into the Hollywood
film *Welcome to Sarajevo*. Also by Michael Nicholson:

Fiction
The Partridge Kite
Red Joker
December Ultimatum
Pilgrim's Rest

Non-fiction
A Measure of Danger
Across the Limpopo
A State of War Exists